P9-ELO-389

"*Call of the Cats* is the most touching, honest, and well-written book I have read in many years. It absorbed me in laughter and in tears and in the acknowledgment of some profound and very human truths. Writing like this does not appear very often, but when it does it touches and delights something very deep within us."

— **Adyashanti**, spiritual teacher, founder of Open Gate Sangha, and author of *The End of Your World*

"Andrew Bloomfield takes us on a journey of the heart that chronicles his unfailing commitment to a colony of feral cats. In a delightfully conversational style, he weaves in fascinating tidbits about the history of cats and his spiritual adventures in India and Nepal. He illuminates invisible strands that bind nature in a neighborhood with modern daily life. Animal lovers will want to savor this fascinating story that gives texture and voice to the mission of caring for untamed creatures who silently live among us."

— **Allen and Linda Anderson**, authors of *Angel Cats* and *Angel Dogs* and founders of the Angel Animals Network

"One might think I would be partial to books about my favorite topic — all things feline, especially wild felines, be they five pounds or five hundred pounds. But that is simply not the case. The truth is, I'm only interested in books that are extraordinarily well written, and I find them to be few and far between. A poorly written book, even about cats, would leave me, well, cat-atonic. Great writing is great story-telling, and Andrew Bloomfield is a great storyteller. This book is, in a word, stunning! And the fact that Andrew Bloomfield was not a 'cat person' but found his life miraculously transformed by the love of a little feral kitten makes these unpredictable heroes — two- and four-legged alike — totally irresistible. The 'taming' of self-proclaimed narcissist Andrew Bloomfield by a tiny wild female kitten is a captivating read. Buy it for every cat lover you know, as well as every 'not yet' cat lover. If this book doesn't win them over, I don't know what will. Little Tiny's story is a big triumph!"

— **Amelia Kinkade**, author of *Straight from the Horse's Mouth*, *The Language of Miracles*, and *Whispers from the Wild*

"Andrew Bloomfield's *Call of the Cats* is like *Born Free* in an urban back-yard, full of remarkable detail about the wild life around us and the extraordinary emotional attachments that can exist between human beings and the untamed animals that occasionally share our lives. This is a joyful book of spiritual insight and deep human feeling. It will entertain, uplift, and delight."
— **Bruce Joel Rubin**, Academy Award–winning screenwriter of *Ghost, Jacob's Ladder, My Life,* and *The Time Traveler's Wife*

"With humor and wit, *Call of the Cats* illustrates the perils and rewards of rescuing animals that live at the margins of human society. If you have ever cared for an animal, this book will resonate with you."
— **Marty Becker, DVM**, America's Veterinarian and author of *Your Cat: The Owner's Manual*

"Andrew Bloomfield's heartfelt memoir is not just about his uncondi-tional love for the feral-cat colony that he came to know and adopt. It's also a much larger portrait of how we can live with, and gently support, animals, who are all at our mercy."
— **Patrick McDonnell**, creator of *MUTTS* and illustrator of *Guardians of Being*

CALL OF THE CATS

CALL OF THE CATS

*What I Learned
about* LIFE *and*
LOVE *from a*
FERAL COLONY

ANDREW BLOOMFIELD

New World Library
Novato, California

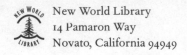

New World Library
14 Pamaron Way
Novato, California 94949

The author's experiences throughout this book are true, although identifying details such as names and locations have been changed to protect the cats and the privacy of others.

Text design by Tona Pearce Myers

Library of Congress Cataloging-in-Publication Data
Names: Bloomfield, Andrew, author.
Title: Call of the cats : what I learned about love and life from a feral
  colony / Andrew Bloomfield.
Description: Novato, California : New World Library, 2016. | Includes
  bibliographical references.
Identifiers: LCCN 2016021610 (print) | LCCN 2016039820 (ebook) | ISBN
  9781608683987 (alk. paper) | ISBN 9781608683994
Subjects: LCSH: Feral cats–California–Los Angeles–Anecdotes.
  | Human-animal relationships.
Classification: LCC SF450 .B56 2016 (print) | LCC SF450 (ebook) | DDC
  636.8009794/94–dc23
LC record available at https://lccn.loc.gov/2016021610

First printing, November 2016
ISBN 978-1-60868-398-7
Ebook ISBN 978-1-60868-399-4

Printed in Canada on 100% postconsumer-waste recycled paper

New World Library is proud to be a Gold Certified Environmentally Responsible Publisher. Publisher certification awarded by Green Press Initiative. www.greenpressinitiative.org

10 9 8 7 6 5 4 3

For my housemates Sophie and Heather,
without whom this adventure never would have been possible.

And for beloved Gumdrop, who passed away
far too young, just before this book's publication.

Contents

"Until one has loved an animal, a part of one's soul remains unawakened."

— ANATOLE FRANCE

"If I ever go looking for my heart's desire again, I won't look any further than my own back yard. Because if it isn't there, I never really lost it to begin with!"

— DOROTHY GALE, *THE WIZARD OF OZ* FILM, 1939

Prologue

When I moved into a modest bungalow in Southern California, I was only vaguely aware that a colony of feral cats inhabited the deep foliage behind my home. Blood-chilling screams of kittens as they were routinely dragged off and devoured by raccoons and coyotes soon made it more than apparent I had inadvertently situated myself at the edge of civilization, the precipice where tame and primal met. I thought I had moved to Mayberry; it turned out to be Wild Kingdom.

Inevitably our worlds would collide. That invisible line of demarcation between us was crossed during a profound and poignant exchange one foggy morning when it became clear I had no choice but to intervene in the bloody drama that was my own backyard.

So began the tumultuous saga of my relationship with this group of skittish, wild, and sometimes fierce felines. I began to name, nurse, feed, house, rescue, and neuter them. Sleep was a rare commodity; I rose from my bed countless times to fend off their attackers. I maxed out credit cards on vet bills and emergency-room visits for myself when mauled by the very cats I was trying to help. Over the years, I became deeply enmeshed in the colony's cycles of births and deaths, rivalries and alliances, cliques and out-casts.

It promised to be a thankless task, with no expectation of reward. The late British writer Alice Thomas Ellis once described such relationships: "There is no reciprocity. Men love women. Women love children. Children love hamsters. Hamsters don't love anyone. It is quite hopeless."

Unlike hamsters, however, the ferals wouldn't allow human touch. They ran from voices or movement. They didn't make eye contact. They didn't purr. These were not strays — abandoned domesticated cats. These were wild animals — untamed and, for the most part, untamable.

This story traces my time-consuming, ruinously expensive, and, in the end, profoundly rewarding twenty-year relationship with a colony of feral cats I came to know and love.

And the irony is, I'm not even a "cat person."

A lovely calico we named Gumdrop.

1 Welcome to LA

When I was seventeen, my mother asked me to drive her to see a psychic in our hometown of Tucson whom everyone was raving about. I had never known my mother to see a psychic and have never known her to see one since. But for some reason, she felt drawn to meet this woman. I waited in a dark overstuffed chair in the living room while Violet gave Mom her reading in the next room. I could see them huddled together but, despite my best efforts, couldn't make out any words until Violet stopped midsentence, looked over my mother's head at me, and blurted, "You know, your son's going to Hollywood. And he's going to find his true calling there."

Well, then I knew for sure she was a fake, and I walked out to the car to wait for my mother, determined not to spend another moment in that deluded woman's home. Hollywood! I couldn't believe Mom was in there paying real money for such crap. I had, somewhat inexplicably, set my sights on the Far East and would spend hours in the library poring over picture books of the Himalayas. Not long after, I found myself living in Nepal, spending the better part of two years researching a seventeenth-century pilgrim's guidebook and traipsing across the Himalayan foothills exploring the route described in it, as part of my Asian studies undergraduate degree. Hollywood was the last place on my mind. And yet it is where I eventually landed after all.

After Nepal, I opened a bookstore in Seattle but left it behind to work for an astrologer in Los Angeles. It started out grand. My first LA experience was at daybreak, a few blocks from Santa Monica Beach. A quiet and serene Sunday. I sat on a bench, watching dawn colors toy with wispy clouds. I'm going to like it here, I thought. Then, in the distance, I heard the squealing of tires and a car engine being pushed beyond its limits. I saw a small red Toyota coming my way whip around the corner, jammed to the gills with desperate- and dangerous-looking men. Behind them raced five squad cars, sirens blaring.

I couldn't believe my luck. They were shooting a movie right where I sat! The red car kept going around in circles while being chased by the cops. Then one of the men positioned himself out the Toyota's rear window and aimed his gun at the pursuing police cars. Seeing the gun, the driver of the patrol vehicle veered out of the way, sideswiping the car parked in front of me. An officer from the passenger side leaped out and pulled me to the ground, yelling, "Get down, you idiot! They just robbed a bank!" That's when it dawned on me. I hadn't seen any cameras or production crews. I just assumed everything about Los Angeles was movies.

It was my first lesson that the veil between real and make-believe was paper thin in this town.

The following evening, I made my first pilgrimage to the Sunset Strip. I passed the location of the old Cafe Trocadero, an upscale nightclub once frequented by major stars and host to Saturday night high-stakes poker games between studio moguls. I walked by the Roxy and Whisky a Go-Go, and crossed the street to see what had once been the Melody Room, where Mickey Cohen and Bugsy Siegel ran a gambling parlor. I walked by the slab of concrete where River Phoenix died of an overdose. Then slightly up the hill past cofounder Elton John's Le Dome restaurant.

Crossing La Cienega Boulevard, I approached the Mondrian Hotel, where a tuxedo-clad security guard whisked me through a side door. I was hurried past the luxurious pool and led upstairs to the grand opening of the Sky Bar. I suddenly found myself at a table, sitting across from Adam Sandler, who was enjoying a cold bottle of beer, Jean-Claude Van Damme, two coked-out producers with white flake residue on their faces, and two enormously buxom blondes who kept lifting their shirts high over their heads, exposing their naked breasts to revelers by the pool below.

After leaving the Sky Bar, I went next door to the House of Blues. It was jammed with people, and I found myself propelled upstairs and under a red rope into a VIP section. I bumped into a guy who happened to be Sylvester Stallone. He looked over and said, "How you doin'?" as he danced with his wife, Jennifer Flavin. How you doin'? Rocky just said, "How you doin'?" to me? Are you kidding?

People tended to mistake me for a "somebody," and landing in surreal scenes seemed a recurring theme for me. Even Steven Spielberg. We stood outside a karate studio in Brentwood one afternoon, a few feet apart, just the two of us. Apparently his son was in the class, but Steven kept watching me, not his kid. I didn't return the stare, as I felt gaping at celebrities was rude. When

I did glance over, he wore a quizzical look, as if trying to place me. He took a few paces my way, and I said, "I'm sorry, Steven. We've never met." He looked relieved.

Since Violet had proved right about Hollywood, I figured she must be right about my place in the movie business. She said I'd find my calling here, and what else is Hollywood but movies? But I couldn't act, direct, or produce. And I had no contacts. Strolling the Hollywood Walk of Fame one afternoon, gawking like a tourist at each star embedded in cement, I spotted a crumpled flyer for a screenwriting seminar. It read in bold letters, "Want to break into Hollywood? Write a great script!"

I decided the best way to learn to write a screenplay was to read a lot of them. Good ones. I pored over scripts at the Writers Guild and Motion Picture Academy libraries. I wrote scripts. Lots of them. In all genres. I entered screenwriting contests, queried producers, managers, and agents, and attended screenwriting seminars. I soon learned that Hollywood was a closed network. If you didn't know somebody, your screenplay was going to sit in the slush pile, along with the other fifty thousand or so screenplays that are registered with the Writers Guild every year.

I came to realize that my auspicious first days in Hollywood were in fact my peak experience. It all went downhill from there.

After a few years, I was broke and homeless, living in my car. I often parked by the ocean so that when cops came at daybreak, I could feign being a surfer preparing to catch early-morning waves. I huddled around beach campfires at night, joining revelers as if I were part of their group, finding food where I could, usually a plate of beans from a taco truck. I was another Hollywood statistic.

Finally I contacted a woman I had dated after first arriving in LA. I used to visit Sophie and had become friendly with her sister, Heather, with whom she shared a 1930s bungalow ten miles from downtown. Hearing of my predicament, Sophie and Heather offered me their sofa for a few days.

That lumpy sofa felt like the Ritz. I couldn't fully relax — I was used to sleeping with one eye open, wary of thieves and cops — but what a relief it was to have someone offer refuge when every door had seemingly been shut in my face. I reassessed my life while living on that couch and decided to get back to basics. Write what you know, screenwriting instructors always said. Well, I knew something about Asia. So when I stumbled across the true story of a smuggler whose life was transformed by a chance meeting with a Tibetan lama, I thought I had hit pay dirt.

I borrowed money to fly to San Francisco and meet with this smuggler in person. After several days spent recording his story, I felt fully in my element. Returning to Southern California, I felt enthusiastic for the first time in years. About the project, certainly, but also about my upgraded living quarters. Noticing how well the three of us were getting along, the sisters suggested we should be housemates. They offered me their spare room, and I gratefully accepted. Now that I had a safe place to stay, I could also practice astrology, which I had been introduced to years before. Reading astrological charts was a way to help pay my share of the rent and utilities. And ironically enough, it would prove a way into Hollywood. Within a few months, some of my clients included executives at the very studios I was trying to impress as a screenwriter.

After my San Francisco trip, my head was swimming with ideas for the potential film project. Needing some fresh air and wanting to stretch my legs before starting what I was sure would be my breakthrough screenplay, I opened the back door and walked into the yard. I was brought to a standstill by the sight of a dead kitten.

During the time I had dated Sophie, and even more since moving in, I had become aware of a large feral-cat colony that haunted the lush boundary between the sisters' backyard and the neighbor's yard beyond. The cats were a myriad of colors, shapes, and sizes. They were stealthy and skittish, shadows at night, ghostlike flashes in the trees, peering under the high wooden fence that separated our yards.

Occasionally I would spot a startled eye, a black nose, a wispy tail through the broken slats in the fence. The felines were as wary of human contact as any wild animal. Though to the untrained eye some might be mistaken for domesticated house cats, they were unequivocally feral.

I came to learn that their predators, coyotes and raccoons, lived in the latticework of dried arroyos that ran down out of the San Gabriel Mountains. And they knew where to come for fresh meat. Newborn litters and young kittens were particularly vulnerable. Their numbers would grow and then diminish. We reasoned — albeit uneasily — that this was nature at work and none of our business. The cats had been there before the sisters moved in and would probably outlast them.

On the other hand, the creatures looked half-starved and desperate. After watching, helpless, as a delicate white cat choked to death on a bone she had scavenged from a neighbor's trash, we felt we had no choice. We took to putting out food to ensure the felines had some type of decent nourishment (and then cleaning up after every feeding so as not to attract other wildlife).

I remember Heather standing with a handful of cat food for nearly half an hour, absolutely frozen, unable to place the food outside because she understood the ramifications of getting involved at that level. Soon we'd begun feeding what we assumed was a population of about fifteen cats twice a day, morning and night. Then we began naming the cats in order to keep track of their number. Despite these interventions, we were determined not to get any more involved. Sophie and Heather both worked full-time and enjoyed busy social lives. We were all basically self-absorbed — single and childless. And we weren't, by any stretch, cat lovers.

The dead kitten at my feet was a stunning mix of tortoiseshell and tabby markings, patches of chocolate and cinnamon melded with royal-orange stripes down her legs that would've made her lion ancestors proud. Just the day before, I'd observed this little sprite dancing with joy in the backyard, spinning and leaping in air, the enthusiasm of life surging through her tiny body. As my gaze lifted from the lifeless creature, I saw eight feral cats looking up at me. They sat on their haunches in a perfect semicircle, each so quiet and perfectly positioned it seemed as if someone had hand-placed them.

I recognized these cats: there was Caliby, Snow White, Crazy Calico, Shadow, Beige, Juniorette, Baby Gray, and Marble. Two males and the rest females, ranging in color and appearance from pitch black to Siamese. I was stunned that they were out in the open and not fleeing from my presence. More significantly, each cat stared me dead in the eye. As I turned my head to look at each animal, it would fiercely hold my gaze. This feral cats do not do.

Something was happening here. Something big. I became nervous. This had all the familiar earmarks of the universe stepping in to supplant my personal plans. Though I knew it was nobler to put another being's concerns ahead of my own, I rarely had the inclination to truly do so. Putting out food was one thing, but real commitments eluded me. Yet I felt that these cats were asking for my help. I looked down at the carcass, and their eyes followed mine; and then I looked back at them, and they held my gaze again. Are you sure you have the right guy? I wondered. Did they, too, think I was somebody I wasn't?

I tried choking back the tears running down my face as I contemplated the radiant spirit that, only the day before, had animated this kitten but now had departed, leaving her cold and still. It seems clichéd, but I wondered about a world where in one moment delicate, innocent beings expressed life with carefree abandon and in the next were viciously struck down. By what or whose design?

I remembered attending, some years before, a talk the Dalai Lama had given. Suddenly, in the middle of it, he began to weep. I thought at first he was laughing, as he is known to do. But then I realized he was crying. The audience sat in stunned silence. Then cries turned to sobs, and he seemed inconsolable. After some time, he blew his nose and wiped his eyes and continued his spiritual discourse. I found out later a close friend of his had died shortly before his talk. At the time, I reflected on the difference between contemplating death intellectually and having your heart torn apart by it in real life.

As I crouched next to the kitten, wiping my tears, I noticed she had suffered a violent death. She had been disemboweled; blood was splattered across her singular markings; a paw was missing. The circle of cats came close as I examined her body. Then I sat down on the ground and took a deep breath. When I exhaled, the animals recoiled as if to run but held fast. I addressed the group with my gaze, turning my head to look at each quivering creature before finally saying aloud, "Okay, I'll help." Maybe Violet had been right. I had found my true calling in Hollywood.

A feral in the tree.

2 It Begins

When I was growing up, my family had dogs. Big ones. My father was allergic to cats. That didn't stop my younger sister, who loved all living creatures, from bringing home a stray feline she named Rifka. Seeing how much distress the cat caused my father, my mother promptly tossed it out back. Our yard was overgrown with plants and trees, and my parents figured the cat would find plenty there to keep her occupied. She would eventually be given to a friend for care, but not before giving birth to a litter survived by a single male, a cat my parents named Pifka (yes, my parents really are that funny).

After my time in Asia, I returned home and rented a small cottage near the house I grew up in. I thought it might be nice to have a cat for company, and I spent hours in my parents' backyard looking for the legendary Pifka, spawn of Rifka, who they were sure was "back there somewhere."

I imagined how this goblin might look after years of being alone in the "wilderness." I pried under bushes, took apart the woodpile one log at a time, and poked under the old playhouse, until finally I spotted what looked like a matted weed. Except that it moved.

As I came closer, it moved faster, and away from me. I couldn't stop laughing. Unable to locate his head, eyes, or any other part of him, I saw this scurrying matted blob as more cartoon creature than cat. I bought an animal trap and patiently waited several days, hoping the aroma of the salmon I used for bait would be so inviting that the little guy just wouldn't be able to resist. One afternoon, I saw the piebald mound slinking toward the trap. Given the full head of Rastafarian locks he was sporting, he was surprisingly spry. He gingerly entered the trap, grabbed the fish (ah, I thought, that's where his mouth is), then started backing his way out, but the fish fell apart. He lunged for the largest piece and stepped on the trigger. *Wham!*

I've never seen anything quite like what happened next. That cage jumped around the patio like it was spring-loaded. Banshee screams accompanied its dance, and had there been YouTube then, I'm sure this bouncing, shrieking cat cage would have received millions of hits. I managed to maneuver the trap into the backseat of my car and sped off toward my cottage. In my rearview mirror, the trap bounced up and down and smashed against the doors. I prayed it would hold; I didn't want to think what might happen should this maniac get loose.

Once I arrived home, I placed the cage in my enclosed yard and carefully opened its door, then sprinted across the yard.

Nothing happened. The cat just lay there, flat on his belly, completely inert. Figuring the poor guy had had enough excitement for one day, I left food and water by the cage and went inside. The next morning, nothing had changed. The moving weed continued to cower; the food and water remained untouched.

The following day, however, the cage was empty. And though I didn't see the cat again until days later, I did notice that the food and water I put out were being consumed.

The weeks went by, and I'd observe him watching me from afar. If nothing else, my time in the East had taught me patience (ever try boarding a local train in Mumbai during rush hour?), and I made a practice of never making eye contact or letting on that I was aware of him.

The heat was extreme that summer, and I'd spend every evening seated on the cottage roof for hours on end to cool down. One night I spotted the beast — by now he was too unkempt to call a cat — sharing the roof with me, sitting on the edge, in the farthest corner. In fact, I'll bet that half his body was hanging over the edge, twelve feet off the ground. As days went by, I noticed that ever so slowly, inch by inch, he was seating himself closer to me. I made a point of leaving my arms draped over my knees and my hands extended in case he wanted to make contact, but I never reached for him.

Then the moment came, like being in high school and finally winning over the person you've had a crush on since first grade. The beast pushed his head against my hand and then lay down next to me. It's an ineffable feeling, the warmth of being accepted by another living creature.

Our nightly routine became sitting together on the roof, listening to crickets, his right hook lashing out at the occasional bug flying by. Before long, this wild creature that had never known human touch would curl himself into my lap and sleep. Eventually he felt comfortable enough to enter the cottage and even began sitting on my bed. At first, in typical fashion, he perched on the farthest corner. Over time, he moved closer and closer to me, until one night he crept onto the pillow next to mine.

In time, we became very close, and I was able to cut the weeds from his coat and brush out his hair. Even then, I wouldn't have described Pifka as domestic. He was wild at heart, playing nice. And he reminded me of this at random times when, for no apparent reason, he would suddenly leap onto my chest, grab my jugular between his teeth and bite down, applying pressure like a skilled assassin, letting up just before drawing blood, all the while screaming his terrifying wail.

The only other overt sign of his wildness would occur whenever someone would visit. Hearing footsteps approaching, he would run for his life, hurling himself against the closest window with all his might, trying to smash his way to freedom. Think the Cowardly Lion fleeing down the long hallway from thundering Oz, veering off and diving through the stained glass window. When I eventually left the cottage, the new tenant, who was a friend of mine, devoted herself to the cat, and they got on famously.

I wasn't a cat person.

Several years before I moved into the Southern California bungalow, my housemates had also heeded a call from the wild — and they weren't cat people either. It was late summer, and a huge storm blew in late one afternoon, the wind fierce and howling. Sophie and Heather heard what they thought sounded like distressed meows. They listened carefully but determined that it was just the wind. No, there it was again, the tiniest mewing sound.

They rushed outside but couldn't locate the kitten. The calls seemed to be coming from the mini jungle in the yard adjacent to theirs. They climbed the fence but still couldn't locate the kitten. It was getting dark, due to both the hour and the gathering storm. Bolts of lightning struck, large bursts of wind swept through, and the meows grew more frantic.

The sisters ran outside, down the sidewalk, and around the block to the neighbor's home and knocked on the door. An elderly Chinese couple answered, not speaking a word of English. Heather and Sophie gestured toward the bushes, pantomiming a cat's ears and whiskers. The couple didn't understand, and they were not amused. As the sisters became more animated, the couple became more withdrawn.

The sisters were determined to snatch the kitten, but the couple began shouting at them. Then the couple's son appeared in the doorway, and he spoke a few words of English. He translated to his parents what Heather was saying, and they agreed to let him lead the sisters into their backyard. By now, the storm was raging. They searched everywhere to no avail. Then, in a lull, the faintest sound of mews could be heard. The young man followed the noise, looked inside a large tumbleweed, and there, in the center of this natural womb, sat a little tabby kitten, shaking and terrified.

The man snatched the kitten, dangling it in the air, the fierce wind blowing its body to and fro, the kitten meowing louder than ever now.

"What are you going to do?" he yelled over the wind at the sisters.

Heather and Sophie just stared at each other, not knowing how to answer. The old couple started yelling from the background.

"They want you to leave," he said. "What are you going to do? C'mon!"

Sophie yelled to Heather, "Make sure it's a cat!"

"Of course it's a cat!" she shouted back.

"C'mon!" the man yelled again. Heather reached out, grabbed the cat, and tucked it into her palm.

As the sisters turned the corner for home, a bolt of lightning hit a transformer above them that rained down sparks. Both screamed, while Heather held the kitten tight. They burst into the house, only to find the power out. Not able to find any candles, they jumped into the car and rushed to the closest vet. He examined the kitten and determined it was a male feral who had been well taken care of and fed by his mother. The vet said the kitten was about ten days old and they could expect his eyes to open in a few more days. He gave them a formula bottle and a soft blanket and sent them on their way.

The sisters speculated that the matriarch of the colony inhabiting their yard, a cunning Siamese feral they'd named Grande Dame, and the alpha male, an orange tabby they called Morris, were the kitten's parents. Since it was August, Heather named the kitten Leo. And he would spend the rest of his sixteen-year life with her. She kept him indoors, knowing that predators would make short work of him, and later moved him into her room when another rescued cat we brought inside caused Leo too much stress. Though raised in domesticity since a newborn, Leo was still a few generations from tame; in all the years I knew him, any attempt I made to pet him resulted only in thrashing claws and hissing. As much as he trusted Heather, even she wasn't completely immune to his ferocious lashings.

There were moments of calm, especially when he was young. I remember the time he crawled up my arm, burrowed under the sleeve of my shirt, and curled up and went to sleep in the hollow of my collarbone. When Heather went to work, she would drop him off at what she called "baby daycare." This meant her parents' house.

Her parents were none too pleased when they first heard of

this plan, and it led to a huge fight. Her mother refused to let that cat in her house. Heather was somewhat surprised by this, as she'd expected that her father would protest louder. Heather stood outside the door, Leo in his box, her mother pushing her away, but her father just looked around the corner, curious. Finally realizing Leo would die if not watched over, her mother relented. And by the end of the day, Heather's mother didn't want to let him go. Now her parents looked forward to baby daycare. Except that Leo would terrorize the males in the house: Heather's father and brother. They couldn't walk past the cat without getting attacked, claws and all. At times, Leo would lie in ambush on the refrigerator, just waiting for one of them to walk by. This was not domestic cat play; this was serious. Like living with a ninja.

So when I came to live with Sophie and Heather, there was one male cat in the house. And then me. It was the calm before a storm of cats came into our lives.

Tiny under a blanket,
resting against my toe.

3 Tiny: A Kitten in the Fog

I 've heard it said that you don't choose your pet; it chooses you. Leo chose Heather; and now I, too, was about to be chosen. One summer evening, a dense fog rolled in from the ocean, creeping over LA. Heather banged pots and pans in the kitchen, preparing dinner. Sophie and I watched TV from the living-room couch. Over the household noise, we heard a strange sound. We turned off the television and listened. Yes, there it was again — a small, anguished, forlorn cry. A kitten in distress, crying for us, it seemed. It's like when kids are outside playing and you can locate your child's voice amid the cacophony because it is just so recognizable. Our nights were often punctuated by howls, meows, and cries. But this was different. I listened intently. This wasn't so much a cry for the ears; it was a cry for the heart. I literally felt my heart vibrating with each shrieking call. And yet, I'm ashamed to admit, I did nothing.

The weak cries went on all night. I know because I didn't sleep. I listened, tense, almost pleading for the sounds to continue, fearful what it would mean if they stopped. Finally, at daybreak, I couldn't take it anymore and followed the sounds to the side of the house. Tucked between a trash can and a recycling bin was a tiny, hairless kitten. It seemed inconceivable that it had survived the cold, damp night. No more than three inches long, small enough to cup in my palm (though I didn't touch it), it wriggled on its side, now strangely silent, eyes closed, minute ears pinned back against its delicate head, minuscule limbs flailing. I was struck by how ruthless nature could be, that it could deposit into the wild a creature so small it would barely whet the appetite of predators. Or perhaps I was being shown how courageous nature was — that the possibility of survival still existed, even against those odds.

My housemates joined me.

"Oh my god, we have to do something," gasped Heather.

"We are *not* bringing it inside!" Sophie said, knowing what her sister was thinking.

"It's going to die out here!"

"It survived the night. The mother must be nearby."

"We don't know that."

I grew up with two sisters and knew better than to get in the middle of a sisterly dispute. Still, I was about to intercede, when a small tortoiseshell female, whom we had seen before with kittens, slipped in from beneath a rotted board in the nearby fence, plucked up the kitten by its nape, and scurried away.

"Told you!" Sophie said, with more than a hint of triumph in her voice.

"Then why was it crying all night?" Heather countered. She was not quite convinced. And neither was I.

The sisters went inside to get ready for the day. But I couldn't move. I hope my female readers won't feel I'm being presumptuous when I say I felt like a woman who has accidentally become pregnant and is surprised by an unshakable certainty that she is going to keep the baby. I suddenly felt irrevocably attached to this tiny creature. I knew in that instant the kitten was my responsibility and that I would move heaven and earth for it — a shocking revelation, really, given how narcissistic I had been most of my life.

I wondered why such feelings surged inside me when this kitten was obviously being cared for by its mother. Hearing the scratching of claws on the back fence, I saw the black-and-gray tortie reappear, the tiny kitten in her mouth, before leaping into the dense foliage, hopefully moving her kitten to safety. What a relief, and none too soon, as I had to prepare for a phone call. In a few hours, I was scheduled to speak with a prominent studio head — who had somehow caught wind of my project — while he drove to a golfing weekend in Palm Springs.

The call went better than expected. I pitched him the story of the smuggler, and he described it as "the most exciting thing I've heard in eons." I was still too green to realize that this was Hollywood-speak — the reflex of hyperbole and fabrication that is part of the business. I hung up the phone glowing, the kitten temporarily forgotten. My focus had reverted to me and my impending breakthrough into the capricious world of entertainment.

Later that evening, an ominous hush once again fell on the house. Peering through the blinds, I saw that the thick fog had rolled back in, pushing up against the glass. And, as in a scary movie where the ghost begins to haunt at the appointed hour, the kitten's cries began again.

Boy, did that kitty have lungs! Lights flicked on in nearby houses; neighbors came out to investigate. Whenever someone approached, the kitten would fall silent and remain hidden. But if it heard the sisters or me come out of the house, it screamed at the top of its lungs and wiggled on legs no longer than those of a mouse into the open to be seen.

Another sleepless night. We periodically ventured outside to check on the kitten. Newborns are fodder to the city's wildlife, and the last thing we wanted was a kitten advertising itself. Each time we went out back, the mother was seemingly caring for it.

The next morning, we were frazzled wrecks. During the day, when Sophie and Heather were out, the now-familiar cries began again. I hurried outside and watched as the mother cat grabbed the kitten by the neck, knocking its head into fence posts as she trotted away. She soon returned, dangling the kitten like a worthless handbag, put it down, seemed to forget about it, then rushed back and snatched it up again. Her maternal instincts seemed to flip on and off like a switch. Given her careless approach to parenting, if there had been any other kittens in the litter, they were no doubt long gone from this world.

That evening, all was quiet on the kitty front. Too quiet. We went out to take a look. Not five steps from the back door, we found the kitten wallowing in the dirt, eyes pinched shut, ears pinned back, four legs flailing. It heard our steps and started to cry. We waited for its mother to return. The cries became weaker and weaker. I wanted to touch the kitten to reassure it but didn't want my scent on its body, fearing that would be the last straw for what was clearly an ambivalent mother.

Heather felt she had to do something. She scooped up the kitten with a piece of cardboard and moved it against the fence, where it would be better shielded by plants and trees. Just then the mother appeared and picked up the kitten, dropped it quickly, and dashed off without it.

It seems incredible now that we basically did nothing for the kitten except obsess about it for *the next two days*! We debated endlessly. What convinced us not to intervene was that the mother seemed to be trying to care for it, no matter how recklessly. There are lots of reckless mothers out there, we figured. And not just in the animal world!

At the end of the second day, Sophie, who had been adamantly opposed to becoming more deeply involved (wisely sensing the slippery slope we were on) came around. We decided to step in. But we couldn't find the kitten! There was no sign of it anywhere. My heart raced, and I became flooded with guilt as we scoured the backyard. With every passing minute, my stomach knotted tighter at the prospect of finding a lifeless body. After searching for hours, we spotted its wrinkled, hairless body in the place we called the "Four Corners," where the fences of Samoan, Hispanic, and Chinese neighbors met ours.

Face down in the dirt, the kitten emitted a choking moan, its body oddly flat, like a large fava bean. It was clearly close to death. We carefully placed it in a box and rushed to the closest emergency vet.

The veterinary assistant asked for a name as she filled out paperwork. "Tiny!" Heather blurted out.

It seemed we had a female calico, which the assistant determined from the markings on the kitten's skin. As the vet examined her, Tiny rolled into the large folds of his gentle hands, her ears pressed back, her tongue trying to locate sustenance from thin air. It was unlikely, he pronounced, that Tiny would survive another few hours. He didn't think she had been getting any nourishment from her mother, and she was severely hypothermic. There was really nothing he could do. Sophie, Heather, and I looked at each other, crushed by the realization of how wrong we had been. Tiny had essentially been abandoned at birth.

With the tacit understanding that Tiny would likely be dead in hours, we determined to do everything we could to comfort her. Euthanasia never crossed our minds. We raced to the pet store, bought kitten formula and droppers, hurried home, and made Tiny a nice warm bed with soft towels over a heating pad. But she was too weak to feed. Not a drop of formula passed her lips. Inert, eyes closed, she was barely breathing. There was nothing to do except keep Tiny as warm as possible. We took turns holding her blanket-shrouded body against ours. Heather suggested letting the warm formula dribble down between our fingers to see if she might lick it. Perhaps the feeling of skin and warm milk against her lips would make her react as she would to a teat.

We warmed the formula and ever so slowly let a minute stream dribble down the crease in Heather's fingers to Tiny's mouth. The kitten instinctively stuck out her tongue. Euphoria! She tasted a little more. Then more. When we deemed she'd had enough, the sisters left for bed, and I kept watch. I felt myself begging her to take another breath. I willed her diaphragm to continue to rise and fall.

Willing Tiny to survive reminded me of my family dog, Harley, a beautiful Great Dane–German shepherd mix. As sometimes happens with large dogs, Harley stood up from an awkward position one evening, and unbeknownst to us, his stomach folded onto itself. It was late on a Sunday. My sisters and I were pre-teens, and my father, a physician we depended on for all things medical, was out of town. Our cheerful, affectionate, robust dog panted, drooled, stumbled, and whimpered. My mother felt it was something that might remedy itself on its own. Harley tried to drink water and find a comfortable position. He twisted, turned, and was clearly in great pain. He finally collapsed on his side and weakly licked my hand.

Hour after hour, one breath at a time, I watched him breathe. Mom said we would take him to the vet in the morning if he was still ailing. That meant all I needed was for his chest to keep rising and falling through the night. The hours passed. It was my first experience of ferociously willing life to continue. I don't remember falling asleep, but I woke up at daybreak, my face against his. I waited to feel his breath against my cheek. Nothing. His chest was still. I knew he was dead, although his body was still soft and warm.

The grief I had felt at losing Harley contributed to the urgency I felt to comfort this dying kitten. I couldn't bear the idea of losing another animal in my care.

Tiny stayed in my room. Every few hours, I offered her formula, then closed the flaps to the box we had made to keep in the heat. When the sun rose, I heard a small stir, and I knew she had survived.

"She's alive!" I called out.

Sophie and Heather bounded into the room. Clearly, nothing was more important than Tiny surviving the night. It dwarfed whatever individual dramas we were stewing over. There's something about a crisis that can bring clarity. You see what's important and what isn't. And basically everything you thought was important turns out not to be. There comes a relief in not self-obsessing, and completely giving yourself to another being in need, without expecting anything in return. I once heard a spiritual teacher say that the mantra of stupidity is "What about me?" At last I had an inkling of what he meant.

We kept Tiny warm and continued to feed her formula through our fingers, cautiously optimistic that we were over the hump. Over the next few days, bristles of white, brown, and orange fur appeared on Tiny's bare paws. It sprouted so quickly it seemed to emerge right before our eyes. We created a spreadsheet for her twenty-four-hour care. Each of us recorded what we did and for how long, whether it was keeping Tiny company, warming her against our bodies, feeding her, or rubbing warm compresses on her to assist with elimination, approximating the warm tongue of her mother.

When she became stronger, I took her to a nearby animal

hospital. A large boil had formed on the side of her neck, an infected sore we thought had been caused by her mother's teeth repeatedly grabbing her scruff. We also wanted an overall assessment of her progress.

The clinic staff, smitten, gathered around to marvel at Tiny. Then the head assistant appeared and glanced into the box, trying to wipe the spontaneous smile from her face and be stern. "Lots of people bring us abandoned cats," she explained. "And they leave them here. We won't accept this cat if you're going to desert her." She looked me straight in the eye. "Are you willing to take full responsibility for this cat? Not only for the current services, but for the rest of her life?"

I felt as though I were at the altar, at one of those crossroads in life when you sense that the next moment will forever change things as you know them. A gesture of sacrificing your personal agenda for something bigger, a responsibility that so fully blocks your path, it's impossible to step around it, one that presses itself right up against your face so it's impossible to deny it's yours. Overwhelmed by the enormity of what I was agreeing to, but unable to stop myself, I blurted out, "Yes! I do! I do!"

Everyone was all smiles. I felt like I had passed a test that most fail. Almost as soon as those words had left my lips, a flash of remorse, like ruing a shotgun Vegas wedding, hit me. Cats can live upwards of twenty years, and I wasn't sure I could even afford the vet bill for this visit. I rifled through my wallet to see if any of my credit cards still looked good.

The vet entered and pierced the boil with a lance. He wrapped it and then examined Tiny carefully. His look turned dour. "Well, I'm sorry to say I'm quite certain she has brain damage," he told me. "Besides the exposure, she just didn't get the nourishment she needed. You're lucky she survived at all. They usually don't."

My head fell to my hands. I was speechless. Brain damage? My only concern until that point had been getting her to eat.

"And she'll likely never regain the use of her back legs," the vet added.

We had noticed she had no function there. Whenever she would move, she would drag her back legs behind her.

"Other than that, I think she'll survive," he concluded. "But a brain-damaged cat will need extra care and protection. Are you willing to help?"

I nodded. I had made my vows, and I fully intended to keep them.

Two teenage feral offspring.

4 Rehab

Rehab is an LA cliché, but this kitten did not go off to some swanky ranch in Malibu to get her head straight. No, she stayed with me in my modest room as I pecked away on my laptop, trying to manufacture the visions and dreams and high-concept twenty-word pitches I prayed would interest mercurial studio executives, mercenary independent producers, and beautiful, narcissistic rising stars.

As I sat with Tiny for hours every day, nursing her and watching her grow, I had to admit to myself that I'd always had a soft spot for lost, dispossessed, starved, half-wild animals. Years earlier, when I had been living in a Nepali village, I was met one morning by a very pregnant dog that had collapsed on my veranda. She was a lovely, short-coat brindle hound, and starving.

As you might imagine, dogs didn't have it easy in an impoverished nation like Nepal. I cooked up food and hand-fed her, just as I was doing for Tiny. The pregnant hound stayed on my veranda for weeks, those deep brown eyes soulful and sweet. She started to regain her strength but still enjoyed being hand-fed, so much that she would pretend she was still weak just so I would continue passing food from my fingers to her mouth. I knew it was an act because her spirited tail thumped with great vigor and as soon as she ate she would leap up and run in circles of joy.

She gave birth to two robust males, one jet black, the other brindled. They were impressive in stature, attracting the attention of passersby, who would stop to admire them. At night, the young hounds stood guard like Fu dogs, one on each side of my door. One day, I heard a commotion and saw two Tibetan nomads running down the path away from my house, each carrying one of my dogs under their arm. It wasn't easy getting onto my veranda — you had to enter through a locked gate and pass the homes of two other families. I ran downstairs after the bandits, admonishing my neighbors for letting robbers in. They looked baffled. What was I talking about?

I sprinted after the thieves and saw them disappear into the large nomad camp. During winter months, Tibetan nomads descended from the high plateau to feed their livestock on the grass that still grew at lower elevations, and set up camps along the trade route between Nepal and Tibet, in the area where I was living.

The moment I entered the nomads' tent city, the Tibetans were stunned. Westerners didn't enter this place. "Inchi! Inchi!" they called out — "Westerner! Westerner!" I pulled back tent flaps, peering inside, calling for my dogs.

A crowd gathered around me. I foolishly said I was looking for thieves. Well, that was the *wrong* thing to say around a pack of nomads. They pressed toward me, looking none too pleased. An old man intervened and asked me what the problem was. I told him the story, using the Tibetan words "dog friends" (the closest word I knew to *pets*). He laughed, explaining dogs weren't friends. They were *rokpa*s — helpers or servants. If somebody had taken my dogs, it was to protect their tents, he explained. Anyone who was lucky enough to find two big, strong dogs would be using them as guards, not friends. He told me to leave before I got hurt.

I had made the mistake of raising the dogs as I would have in America, making them friendly, not vicious. They were coddled, and territorial only at night. The nomads had seen they were friendly and just grabbed them. They had a better use for these robust creatures than just letting them sun themselves on my veranda.

As I went home empty-handed I considered what the old man had said. And it came back to me as I watched over Tiny, my brain-damaged feral kitten with no use of her back legs. Maybe I was too indulgent. This was, after all, a wild cat. A friend of mine grew up on a farm in Indiana and owned Siamese cats. Yet he never used the word *pet* to describe them. These weren't your lap-cat, dining-on-silver-plates Siamese. These were scar-faced, shoulders-as-large-as-a-prizefighter's Siamese. He explained that everything on his farm had a purpose, including the cats. Theirs was to hunt prairie dogs. They'd haul them from their holes and heave them into the back of the Ford F-150 pickup, then paw at them in play before slaughtering them. The cats never entered the house, and they were never coddled.

For much of human history, and still today in many places, animals were considered tools. But that kind of utility has become complicated, and is largely inapplicable, in the case of our closest domesticated animals: dogs, horses, and, of course, our little feline friend, the common cat. One line of thinking goes that it wasn't until recently that *pet* in the modern sense, of an animal without a specific function aside from companionship, even entered our lexicon. Animal rights activists argue that the whole idea of a pet is speciesist.

But does that mean the idea of domestication is ethically unsound? What about working animals — are first-world animal activists saying they are obsolete? Or that there was always something exploitative about using animals for our own purposes? I wasn't sure, but watching Tiny sleep made me wonder. Ironically, I felt that she was, in the deepest sense, here to help me. Or perhaps this was yet one more form of self-serving narcissism.

I sat with Tiny for hours, watching her sleep, fantasizing about her becoming healthy, imagining her body covered in luxuriant fur. Even if she had to drag her legs around and was mentally challenged, I reasoned, somehow we could still provide her a comfortable life. At least one in which she would be surrounded by people who loved her. Perhaps my time would've been better spent on an animal more likely to survive. But it came down to feeling over logic. From the first time I heard her cry, I recognized her. Like choosing to save your own child over a stranger's.

Tiny lived in a large box lined with soft blankets, along with a few toys and a heating pad underneath. It was too large for her to climb out of, but she could still prop herself up and peek at me. Her now-opened dark-blue eyes stared at me to no end, and her perky ears were now covered in baby fur. While she slept, I memorized each hair on her body, her every muscle, curve, and nuance. I knew her moods, movements, and gestures.

A certain mew meant she wanted to suckle, not for food, but for comfort. I would give her the meaty flesh of my palm while she kneaded it with her paws, pricking my hand with her delicate little claws. While standing on her two front legs, if she held one of her small paws aloft, it meant she was scared. I made a small cave from her blankets where she could run to hide. Another type of mew meant she wanted to explore, so I lifted her from the box and watched over her as she moved around the room, dragging her rear legs behind her. Heartbreaking — every time.

Feeding now consisted of her grabbing tightly onto my hand while I held the formula bottle for her. Her tiny claws dug into my skin while she sucked so hard on the nipple that she tore holes in it. She could down a bottle of formula in nothing flat and still be hungry. We regulated her intake per the vet's directions, just to be safe. She took in lots of air from gulping so hard and fast at the bottle that I'd have to burp her afterward, holding her against my shoulder and rubbing her delicate back, which she enjoyed, purring the whole time. Sounding like minute hiccups, her burps were small bursts of air between the purrs.

Tiny showed no signs of brain damage but still didn't have the use of her back legs. That didn't keep her from trying. She'd scratch at the sides of her box, trying to boost her body up. One afternoon when she was several weeks old, I heard her gagging and quickly pulled her from the box so she could retch. As soon as she was done, she looked up at me, eyes twinkling. I felt a palpable bond the likes of which I'd never experienced before — a deeply protective, nurturing parental instinct. Growing up, I had always assumed I would have children. But not having found a partner or opportunity for marriage, I had long since put the idea of a family of my own out of my mind. I know it may sound ridiculous, but I suddenly felt like a father.

My housemates and I would gently hoist Tiny's body while we stretched out her lame legs, massaging the muscles to encourage blood flow. But when she put weight on her legs, they would collapse. We were undaunted, working her atrophied limbs hour after hour, day after day.

After six weeks, those back legs began showing signs of life. They were wobbly, to be sure, and when she tried to climb the carpeted stairs, she had to work so hard that at the top of each step, she needed to curl up and sleep.

There was something remarkable about her determination and spirit. I came to appreciate these as the very qualities that probably had kept her alive. Perhaps feral cats are more closely aligned with their ancestors in the wild, where the will to live is essential to the survival of the colony.

At night, I kept the lid of Tiny's box partially shut to keep in the warmth. And one night while fast asleep, I was awakened by a *thwack!* And then another *thwack!* I turned on the light, and there was Tiny, beaming at me, wobbling on all fours. She had broken through the lid of the three-foot-high box. Forever. Now she was free to roam and sleep wherever she wanted. And roam she did.

It was one thing to care for Tiny when she was in crisis, but quite another once she was a busy, fully mobile kitten. Putting another being's needs before our own was foreign to my housemates and me. I occasionally heard Sophie yell at Tiny, "Stop following me!"

I once made the mistake of saying, "But she's your baby."

"Don't say that! I'm too busy to be anyone's mother!"

But soon after, I heard Sophie singing softly; I spied her cradling Tiny in her arms and singing Don Ho's "Tiny Bubbles," crooning about feeling "warm all over" and loving her "till the end of time."

My god, I thought, this kitten is turning us all into mush.

Stroking Tiny's soft fur, looking deep into her eyes, Sophie continued, "Did you miss your mommy? Were you a good girl today?"

Soon after Tiny broke free from her box, she could climb the stairs without stopping. First she hopped up and down the stairs like a rabbit, keeping her back two legs together and bouncing. And then, over time, those back legs became strong enough to operate independently of each other. Her fur continued to grow in — white on her chest and chin, while her head, flanks, and legs were a patchwork of oranges, browns, and grays. We tried to cat-proof the house, but to no avail. The stair banister she had recently enjoyed scratching became shredded timber before we had a chance to cover it in towels.

A photographer friend of Heather's visited, and, intrigued with Tiny's beauty, asked if she could photograph Tiny for a series of greeting cards. Seeing the glamour proofs, I couldn't help but marvel that this cat wasn't even supposed to survive.

That will to live, that fight in her, has never left. Her first reaction to anything is to attack. Whenever she is outside, she always has one paw cocked and ready to strike, like a prizefighter's lethal left, just waiting to connect. She shies away from nothing. If something scares her, she runs away and considers a reapproach. The first time she heard the vacuum, she ran for her life; the second time, she held her ground and made us vacuum around her. We hear her seemingly exorcising demons almost daily. She screams and attacks ghosts in midair, nothing visible around her. And we have also learned that if we aren't sensitive to her moods, she can slice and dice with the best of them. One of her nicknames is Shredder, and I have the scars to prove it.

But she has a soft side, too. Every morning, she leaps onto my bed, curls herself into a ball, and lies pressed against my head while I doze. She will stay like that, purring, for as long as I'm there. Often, when she sleeps next to me, she will suddenly bolt up in fear, unsure of where she is. Then she will look over and see my face and feel my hand on her back and relax again, purring, assured that everything is all right and she is safe. I just hope I'll always be there for her in those moments.

When I begin to stir, she knows it's time for her salon treatment. She sprints to the bathroom and jumps onto the sink, admiring herself in the mirror as I brush out her lovely coat, paying special attention to her jowls and the top of her head, places she particularly likes having groomed.

Then, if time permits, we play her favorite game: fishing for kitties. She runs alongside my feet as we race downstairs together, and then I begin trawling the tile floor, dragging a long string with a cat toy attached.

"I wonder if there are any kitties out today."

She stays quiet.

"I hope I catch a whole bunch of kitties today."

And she attacks, grabbing the toy.

"I think I got a bite!"

Then I sweep her up into a deep pillowcase, where she stays very quiet, curled at the bottom.

"Let's see what we've got."

I look in the pillowcase, her bright face looking up at me and meowing playfully.

"Oh look! But this one's too small. We have to return it to the lake."

I scoop her out of the pillowcase, and she meows again playfully, prancing with joy, ready to start again.

Bandy in one of her favorite places.

5 Sleepless in SoCal

"Compassion is not a virtue — it is a commitment. It's not something
we have or don't have — it's something we choose to practice."

— BRENÉ BROWN

T he promise I had made to the semicircle of cats — a tacit agreement that I would care for the entire feral colony for the rest of their lives, come hell or high water — kept me up at night. Not from the death screams of kittens or worrying about Tiny. I wasn't counting sheep; I was counting how many years cats normally live and how old that would make me. Almost any way I figured it, with new kittens arriving every year, I'd be stuck caring for these cats until about fifty years after I was dead. Analyzing anything about one's life at 4:00 AM is a bad idea, as things tend to look ten times their actual size. Yet I knew that in the clarity of daylight a few hours hence, things would still look as bleak as they seemed now.

I sighed, whispering a phrase we often used when we felt overwhelmed by our cat responsibilities: "You've gotta be kitten me." My only chance at sleep was to blame someone. My mother. Yes, of course, my mother. Born to a highly dysfunctional family and suffering severe challenges growing up, she had every reason to be bitter and closed, angry at the world. But instead, she intentionally transmuted the pain of her upbringing to right every wrong she could, by intentionally treating people she encountered, including her children, with patience, respect, and encouragement, and celebrating each of their milestones as if they were her own. (Those admirable qualities were shared by my father and siblings, by the way. Just ask the two grandchildren my parents helped raise.) In every way that her parents and siblings had failed her, she turned those disappointments into opportunities to rewrite history.

Dammit, she made me sensitive to suffering.

She was an artist, and her passion for the deep, hidden, primal aspects of humanity certainly influenced me, too. Her gracious manner belied aspects of my mother's personality that exploded in violent reds, oranges, dark purples, and blacks onto her massive canvases. Her medium was encaustic, which involves melting pigmented beeswax with a torch. Throughout my childhood, I would wake to the smell of propane and melting wax, and explosions of torches being lit, then watch as she entered my room to make sure I was up, a flaming torch in each hand, her smock covered in dripping blood-red and veiny purple wax.

Dammit, she introduced me to the wild.

No wonder, years later, it seemed familiar traversing rural paths in the Himalayan foothills on my way to the burning ghats on cremation days, lured by the putrid smell of burning flesh. Observing bodies engulfed in flame was like sitting at the edge of the world. There I would contemplate death, considering that all of my hopes and dreams will one day go up in smoke, too. Everyone I had ever cared for in the past, or would care for and love in the future, every plan I would ever conceive, every aspiration, my good health and the health of others, would perish. Maybe tomorrow, maybe later, but certain to happen. One of my favorite parables about impermanence was told by the Buddhist monk and teacher Ajahn Chah:

> One day some people came to the master and asked: How can you be happy in a world of such impermanence, where you cannot protect your loved ones from harm, illness or death? The master held up a glass and said: Someone gave me this glass; it holds my water admirably and it glistens in the sunlight. I touch it and it rings! One day the wind may blow it off the shelf, or my elbow may knock it from the table. I know this glass is already broken, so I enjoy it — incredibly.

And my love of animals, well that came from my younger sister, Rachel, dammit, who is no longer living. However, I still seek her wise counsel when in a quandary about animals or about life in general. When we were quite young, my father took my sisters and me fishing, and we caught trout. Rachel stared into the eyes of the trout she caught, into its very soul, and burst into tears. I remember her holding this trout to her chest and sobbing for the rest of the evening, refusing to hand over the fish to be cooked.

I have a vivid memory of her flushed face, her blue eyes swollen shut from crying so hard and long.

Finally my father asked her if she would like to return the fish to the lake, and she nodded emphatically that she would. We all returned to the lake late that night, and he placed the fish back into deep, dark waters. She asked over and over again whether my father had seen the fish swim away, and he said that he had — it had darted quick and fast and sped away. Privately he told me he'd seen it drop like a rock.

My sister influenced me again not long after, when our parents had begun giving us an allowance. All I could think about was spending my newly found riches on comic books and candy. Rachel started receiving newsletters in the mail from the Defenders of Wildlife. At ten years old, she used all her allowance to support a group that protected wild animals. All on her own, without asking for anyone's help or opinion.

And nature respected her for it. This was proved each time we played the game Who Does Tinker Love Best? Placing Tinker, our sorrowful-looking basset hound, equidistant between us, we would do everything in our power to convince him to crawl to us. First looking slowly over to her, then to me, he always, every single time, would lumber over to her, tail wagging, and tripping over his ears. He would receive a huge hug and kiss as a reward. I couldn't even get mad; he made the right choice.

Gosh, I felt better. Obviously I was just an innocent victim of my family of origin. At peace, I finally began to doze off, but then I suddenly jolted awake again, having flashes of old Saturday afternoon movies showing cavemen fighting off bloodthirsty saber-toothed tigers with crude spears. I concluded, in my sleepless delirium, that I was being played, just a pawn in nature's conspiracy to bring enemies together: no way were wild cats and humans meant to coexist.

It turns out my memory was selective, recalling only movies

from the epoch of hunters and gatherers. In fact, the truce took place later, when our societies turned agrarian. After twenty-five million years, cats caught a break in the Fertile Crescent. They migrated from their Asian roots to other places, such as the Americas and Africa, thanks to various land bridges that connected continents, tracts of land that rose and fell according to the whims of the oceans. With an inhale, otherwise submerged dry land would be revealed, allowing passage for many of these four-legged creatures; with an exhale, these isthmuses sank again, trapping others on land they couldn't leave..

The lovefest between human and cat actually began ten thousand years ago and shows no sign of waning. "Eat what you kill," from the hunting-and-gathering period, had become so passé. Now it was the pre-Costco era of storing surplus food. The problem was, stored grain attracted rodents, who not only ate your stash, but spread disease. Lurking behind the curtain, waiting for their entrance cue, was *Felis sylvestris*, the wildcat. Having spent millions of years honing their craft, cats found that capturing rodents in granaries was like taking candy from a baby. Shooting fish in a barrel. Beating a hemophiliac in a bar fight.

So an unspoken pact was established whereby wildcats would have easy access to prey in the granaries, while people would be freed from concern about rodents destroying their stored crops. It was just business.

Or was it?

In my sleepless delirium, I recalled reading about graves discovered in Cyprus and Jericho that revealed that people of prominence were being buried alongside cats about five hundred years after cats and humans first struck that mutually beneficial deal. Perhaps an early indication of cats as pets — or, at the least, of a spiritual connection between the two, because, in the Cyprus case, the cat was young and may have been killed to join the person in the afterlife. Since cats were not native to Cyprus, they must have been brought there on purpose or allowed along for the trip on ships sailing to the island; and being buried with an important human could indicate an emotional connection, not just a functional relationship.

Having solved my personal and historical crises at this ungodly hour, I finally found peace, and hoped that sleep would overtake me. But it did not. The next ghost to appear was a frequent visitor that represented the souls of cats I couldn't save. I was more haunted by the cats I lost than elated by the ones I saved. That last look etched in my memory, those eyes before I'd never see them again. My grasping for a paw just out of reach, their wary look, as they perhaps wondered if it was worth gambling on me rather than staying with what's familiar and succumbing to their fate.

Was it by grace that Tiny survived? Perhaps. It did have that familiar aroma, the same one I'd sensed when I was invited to join my housemates here in this house. When I was feral. When a door literally opened for me that shouldn't have.

I'd smelled that same fragrance once in India. I had left Nepal for India during the summer and spent those months at an ashram during the monsoons. This particular ashram was said to be a place where one's fate could be changed by the power of grace. Something undeserved but still given freely. It could occur in any fashion, they said, but was most obvious when one injured oneself at the ashram. I was told there would be a buzzing of energy around the injured body part, like a swarm of bees or the tingling of bubbles as if champagne had been poured over the injury.

A friend recounted his own experience of grace at the ashram. His life was saved on the day he was to die. For some reason, from the time he was young, he intuitively knew he wouldn't live past age thirty-five. When he slipped on a slab of wet marble at the ashram, splitting open his head on the day of his thirty-sixth birthday, he had the feeling of a swarming of bees around his head (who wouldn't!) and knew this was a sign that his life had been saved.

He left the ashram soon thereafter and, as he boarded a crowded local bus headed for the high Himalayas, prayed not just for an empty seat next to him — that alone would've been a miracle — but also for a fresh copy of French *Vogue* to be there on that empty seat. For some reason he had the deepest wish, from the depths of his soul, to find a copy of that magazine. A fat issue, no less than five hundred pages. And yes, here at this high-altitude provincial bus stop, not only did he discover an empty seat beside him, but there was that fresh copy of *Vogue*, the fall/winter issue, all five hundred pages of it. Grace.

Sounded fascinating to me, and superstitious. But I kept that thought to myself. I had no such experience at the ashram. That is, until the day before I was to leave. My Indian visa was nearing expiration, and I had to hurry for Nepal. I was lucky to have secured the last seat on a bus that would get me there on time, and it was scheduled to leave the following morning. My last afternoon at the ashram, I was helping workers cut down makeshift huts by cutting through the heavy hemp ropes that held them together.

While I was cutting through one remaining cord, an entire wall suddenly fell against me, dislocating my shoulder. The timing couldn't have been worse. But I did feel the champagne tingle and the buzzing around my shoulder, as if someone had applied a warming Tiger Balm poultice to it. Did I really believe it was grace? Umm, no. As far as I was concerned, I was basically screwed.

I reset the shoulder myself and then, early the next morning, hefted my heavy duffels over the good shoulder and trudged from the ashram. I was in considerable pain but figured once I got on the bus, I could just relax. That turned out to be true. I secured an enviable window seat near the front, while a mass of humanity and their farm animals crammed into any available remaining space behind me.

As I left Varanasi, a kaleidoscope of rolling hills highlighted by the afternoon sun unfolded as India passed by in all her rural beauty. After several hours, I stuck my head out the window to get another look at a small *paan* stall we had just passed, which was surrounded by people spitting red juice from their mouths (*paan* is a mixture of areca nut, catechu paste, and slaked lime, all wrapped in a betel leaf, which produces red juice when chewed).

Suddenly there was a thunderous sound, and I noticed a huge slab of metal tumbling behind us. It looked for all the world like a transmission box and finally came to rest in the middle of the highway as our bus slowed to a crawl. Seeing taxis, private cars, motorcycles, and even oxcarts all sliding on a black pool in the road, I realized that it was indeed our transmission, and it had left a huge swath of oil in its wake. Our driver screamed in frustration.

In India, the unexpected is always expected, so this in itself was no surprise. My concern was my quickly expiring visa. I knew that nothing happened fast in India, so I figured it was unlikely another bus would be coming to pick us up anytime soon. I decided to walk back to the *paan* shop we had passed. I spent the rest of the day there, eating *paan mithai* (sweet *paan*) with villagers and enjoying along with them our own private demolition derby each time a vehicle would hit the oil slick, no matter how demonstratively we tried to warn the drivers.

At midnight, I ventured into the fields and took a long bath in a water tank used to irrigate nearby crops. Relaxing with my head against the cement tank while marveling at the ancient Indian night sky overhead, I reflected on a teaching I had once heard — that the world is merely a reflection our own inner state. Fall in love and see how the world looks. If people don't recognize their innate purity, they will live their lives like musk deer, running to exhaustion, frantically searching for that intoxicating scent, without realizing that it originates from themselves. That they are the source of that nectarous aroma.

If you don't understand that, then you'll spend your entire life trying to create ideal situations — the perfect job, the perfect living situation, the perfect relationship — when in fact all you're doing is affecting outer conditions, which, in the end, is like rearranging deck chairs on the *Titanic*. Start with not believing what your mind is telling you, the teacher said. Those thoughts are the false idols; stop worshipping false idols.

Just then, I was startled by the blaring of a bus horn. I hurried back through the crop fields to the road and watched as passengers helped unload the broken bus and reload the new one.

Finally we were off. Settling back into my same window seat and basking in the midnight air, I had to admit — despite my aching shoulder — life was grand. I couldn't suppress the smile on my face. The simple pleasures of life — the *paan* stall, the late-night soak, and now a brand-new bus, going twice the speed of the last one, trying to make up for lost time. I'd be at the border of Nepal with time to spare on my visa, even with the delay.

We drove for hours at breakneck speeds. My sore arm felt best hanging from the window, as the window frame acted as a brace. I'm positively certain I still had that smile on my face when in the next moment, *wham!* A head-on collision with another bus. Bodies flying over seats, mangled metal and broken glass raining over us, unearthly screams, cries, my shoulder, exactly at the point of injury, hurled against the metal flashing in front of me, now a sharp saber since its protective casing had come apart.

I couldn't feel my arm after it was sheared by the metal spear, except what felt like blood pouring from a remaining stub. It wasn't a question of whether my arm was severed; that was a given. It was a question of how much of the arm was left. For the entire time it took to move bodies and shake metal and glass from ourselves, I didn't dare look at my arm, too horrified to see. But then I noticed something familiar. That buzzing and bubbling, the warm Tiger Balm tingle. And I began to wonder. Peering through the smallest slit I could make with one eye, I saw that my arm was still intact.

All I could do was mutter over and over again, each time I inhaled and exhaled, "Thank you, thank you, thank you." Marveling at the miracle of my arm, I almost forgot to pay attention to the most fascinating part of a head-on bus collision in India. The etiquette is this: whichever bus driver can still move must rush into the other bus and beat the tar out of the other driver, even if that driver is dead. This particular accident made it easy since both windshields were shattered and melded together. One merely needed to step over into the other driver's cab and start punching, which is exactly what our driver did to the already unconscious driver of the other bus.

I grabbed my luggage and sat by the road, staring in awe at my intact arm. Sure, I was bruised and bloody, and still chewing on pieces of glass, but it was the arm that amazed me more than anything. People who were still alive and could move sat alongside the road with me; the others were cared for by doctors who happened to be on board. We tried to help but were pushed aside. So there I sat.

Until something snapped inside. Disgusted at being powerless, I had to control my own destiny somehow. No way in hell was I going to wait for another bus. When a local bus crept slowly past the accident site with a placard of a border town, I pounded on its side with all my might until it stopped. I've seen packed buses before, but this was beyond belief.

I dragged my bags over huddled bodies and camped under the metal brace of the dashboard, facing the driver, daring him to say anything. Seeing the look on my face, he just closed the doors, and we drove off. Local buses make many stops and don't travel nearly as quickly as express buses, but it didn't matter to me. I just wanted to be moving.

As the sky lightened and riders slumbered, the driver began to doze, too. I watched him start to nod off, and I realized we were probably going to crash — again. I just wasn't going to let that happen. Feeling around my feet, I found pebbles of various sizes, and for the next four hours, every time I was certain the driver was asleep for good, I flicked a rock at his head. I wasn't a great shot, so sometimes I hit his cheek, occasionally his eye, his forehead, his chest. And each time, he would straighten up and continue driving, as if he'd just been given a shot of espresso.

We finally arrived at a border town but had to wait all day for a bus going to Kathmandu. An hour before my Indian visa was to expire, I sat perched on the roof of my fourth bus, surrounded by luggage, heading for the Himalayas. I strapped myself in well, given what I'd been through, in case another crash was in the cards. As we passed into Nepal, it happened to be the night of Diwali, the Festival of Lights. As if an exclamation point had been put on the power of grace that saved my arm and perhaps my life, I was welcomed by the entire countryside lit up with candles, villages illumined by thousands of strings of lights, and colored fireworks that continued throughout the night amid a canopy of stars that I marveled at from my front-row seat.

Two colony males.

6 Intervention

Now that Tiny had stabilized, my next priority was figuring out how to protect the colony. It seemed like the
right thing to do, but how could I be sure my involvement would truly be helping rather than harming the colony?
Several things came to mind.

I'd befriended a monk in Nepal who had grown up in a remote
Himalayan monastery. He described the austere conditions of the
monastery as conducive to the lofty spiritual heights they were
able to attain. One day, a Westerner happened on the monastery
and, seeing the conditions there, vowed to help. He arranged for
a water pump system to be installed and also brought electricity

to the monastery. At first, the monks were extremely pleased. But soon the modern conveniences took away the monks' edge. The monk described how he and his fellow monks seemed to lose their drive after that. Life had become easier, and that undermined their motivation. Not long after, most of the monks left, and the monastery eventually became deserted. He concluded that trying to make things better can sometimes make them worse.

I always remembered that. To act, or not to act, that is the question. It reminded me of a Zen teaching I once heard:

> If you go forward, you will lose the essence.
> If you go back, you oppose the truth.
> If you neither go forward nor backward, you are a dead man
>   breathing.
> Tell me, what will you do?

The Bhagavad Gita (as sacred a text for Hindus as the Bible is for Christians) addressed my dilemma of inaction by suggesting that one perform actions without any expectation of reward. Doing the action for action's sake alone is action in its purest form and leaves no residue. That's because pure action just happens. There is no doer, no self-reference. Ask an athlete in the zone — perfection just happens. It's egoless.

I took this to mean that whatever shows up at your front door is yours. Don't overthink it. Artists paint, warriors fight, doctors heal. You got needy cats in the backyard, take care of them. Just don't expect a pat on the back. Seemed the perfect cosmic design for taking care of ferals. No reward expected.

But then I happened on a *New Yorker* cartoon of a lion seated in a living room next to a middle-aged woman. The woman says to the lion, "How do you think I feel when you say those years in the jungle were the happiest time of your life?" And that made me reconsider.

The various ramifications of acting, or not, had my head spinning. I was stuck. But then, at last, things became very clear. What finally stirred me to action was simple. And it boiled down to this: I don't like bullies.

Damn the consequences, I wasn't going to sit around and let predators destroy these cats. Period. Not in my backyard. Not on my watch. I tried amping myself up with these T-shirt slogans, but frankly that didn't help. True, I had made my decision, but I also knew I was way out of my element.

But I decided feeling fear was preferable to feeling helpless. Knowing that a predator was about to attack the colony and there was nothing I could do was about to be excised from my emotional repertoire. One thing I was certain about, however, was that I wouldn't be getting much sleep. Kipling's words ran through my head: "And remember the night is for hunting, and forget not the day is for sleep."

The place to start, I decided, would be to become sensitive to the natural rhythms of my environment. To find a happy medium between imposing myself on my surroundings, which never works out well, and letting nature show me.

Once I got clear, the drama outside morphed into a cartoon in my mind. Greasy-haired raccoons and coyotes with seductive molls on their laps smoked fat cigars, shooting dice in a back alley, cads with scars across their cheeks and eye patches. Cats became helpless, delicate maidens bathing in scintillating rays falling from heaven. And I became Sam Sheepdog from Looney Tunes cartoons, able to pulverize Ralph E. Wolf with a single punch when he threatened my herd.

I continued to indulge, imagining in my Disneyesque fantasy that I would meet a miracle-working vet like Dr. Dolittle, who could magically cure any health issue that might arise for any cat in the colony. Oh, and of course I would win the lottery to pay for it all.

I know it's frowned on to anthropomorphize animals and romanticize the law of the jungle. Ask anyone who's been to Africa on safari or otherwise seen wild animals in their natural habitat. Nature in its most raw is ruthless, violent, devastatingly bloody. That cute bunny rarely gets away from the pursuing fox. The private anguish of slaughter takes place in the shadows, where no one roots for the hunter or laments the fallen. There are no bullies or innocent victims.

Looking at it that way would've been de rigueur here, too. Except that now I was part of the equation. And I believe in intervention when called. When I was quite young, my sister's pet black mice froze solid outside due to an unexpected cold snap, their bodies hard as rocks. My parents were ready to toss them out, but I asked if I might try an experiment first. They agreed. I placed the mice under kitchen heat lamps my mother used to keep food warm, and ever so slowly, like in a children's animated movie, these mice began to move. First their limbs and then the rest of their bodies. And then they opened their eyes. These mice literally came back to life. No vet I've shared this story with over the years has had an explanation, and had my parents and sister not witnessed it, I might not have believed it myself.

Once it became apparent caring for the colony was going to be an around-the-clock endeavor with no pay and few perks, my housemates made it clear to me that their careers came first. They weren't willing for their lives to be usurped by cat responsibilities, and I didn't blame them. As I was the newly minted stay-at-home cat caregiver, the onus was on me.

However, it turned out we did have different ideas about the long-term plan for these cats. One evening, Sophie and I came home only to see Tiny outdoors, hiding under our neighbor's car tire. Obviously relieved to see us, she searched our faces, seemingly wondering whether our feelings toward her had changed. She was clearly experiencing some trauma, as if reliving the days of her early abandonment. I don't know why, but I turned to Sophie and said, "It's like she's having 'Nam flashbacks." But what was she doing outside in the first place?

We carried her inside, and there was Heather in the kitchen. She laughed when she saw us carrying Tiny back into the house.

"Why was Tiny outside?"

"I thought the idea was we get the cats strong and then let them back out."

"Huh?"

"You know, catch and release."

"Not Tiny — after everything she's been through!"

And that's when it struck me: if we didn't have a plan and weren't all on the same page, this could get very tricky.

As it turned out, every case was unique; each cat we helped couldn't be compared to any other. And yet no cat we raised was ever fully returned to the wild. There were several reasons for this. First, they lost their edge. Experimenting by letting the cats out, I noticed they were ignorant of the ways of predators and were basically sitting ducks. Being outside also appeared to create more stress for them. They had to learn about eating with the colony, from the ground rather than bowls, and try to find places to sleep at night that were both somewhat comfortable and safe. And maybe most important, I had fallen in love with them. Having worked hard to get them healthy and strong, I wasn't willing to take any risks with their well-being. Having so little control, I felt whatever amount I did have must be exercised to the fullest.

Once their diet was regulated, I felt my next task was to keep the cats safe from predators. Even before Leo's mother, the Siamese matriarch of the colony, was discovered dead on our neighbor's front lawn, her body viciously mangled, it was clear that predators posed the biggest threat.

I was convinced that if a cat as seasoned and savvy as Leo's mother could be killed, they were all at risk. The first thing I did was have a metal-mesh door installed in place of our solid back door so I could monitor everything happening in the backyard, day or night.

But that wasn't enough. I realized I couldn't fully understand the dynamics outside unless I joined the colony. I began sitting among them, deep in the brush, particularly at night. Thick, musty foliage teemed with life there. Lingering dew and spiderwebs draped around me. Earthy smells wafted familiar, engulfing me like a toddler in the presence of a loving grandfather. Jerusalem crickets, ants, moths, praying mantises, black beetles, ladybugs. Night creatures, no matter how small, came alive. Rustling leaves, unidentifiable chirps and chirrs. I spotted a minuscule baby opossum without its mother. This tiny being defending itself against the elements seemed an impossible feat. Either nature had tremendous faith and courage or it was just plain sadistic. I wasn't sure which. But I did know enough not to bother the creature, as baby opossums make small sneezing sounds to call their mother, which is precisely what happened on this occasion.

How a slice of rain forest ended up in our backyard I'll never know. Passing the house from the street, one would hardly have noticed. But wend along pathways leading to the backyard, and soon you'd realize that sunlight never hit the ground. On a relatively small parcel of land, perhaps twenty by forty feet, large nonindigenous fronds, a myriad of old-growth trees, thick veils of ivy oozing white sap, and deep underbrush drew nourishment from the rich soil. Normal neighborhood sounds dissolved here, replaced with chirps, caws, screeches, and the constant rustling of critters that called it home. Including the feral colony. Had monkeys one day appeared and begun swinging from branch to branch, or the occasional rhino passed by, I would have taken it in stride. The ancient, rotted wood-slatted fence that separated our backyard from our neighbor's had been co-opted, completely absorbed by the wild undergrowth. At times I grasped for the fence only to have it turn to dust in my hands.

During the day, it might seem like an arboretum. But at night, there was the sense that danger lurked at every turn. I carefully studied the cats' reactions to their environment. Some noises warranted no response from them at all. Others, a twitch of the ears, a turn of the head, or a readiness to bolt. While domestic cats might have pounced on surrounding insects, these cats did not, just sitting contentedly until spooked. The main pack sat like bread loaves — or cat loaves, more accurately — a few feet away, their backs to me, indicating trust (if we are to believe cat psychologists).

In time, the colony continued with life almost as if I weren't there. But of course I was, and they were still acutely aware of it. Being ever mindful of their surroundings was essential to their safety. By misreading the terrain, they risked their next step being their last. Death was always close by, and they knew it — just as it is for humans, except that most of us live in denial of that fact. Our egos have us convinced that we're immortal, despite all the evidence to the contrary.

I wouldn't say I was accepted by the colony; I was tolerated. Especially by the main pack, the same cats that had formed the semicircle around the dead kitten, seemingly asking for my help. While I shared close quarters with the cats, what struck me most, besides their constant alertness, was their beauty. Rich coats of pitch black, tiger stripes, Siamese, tortoiseshell, gray, white-and-orange tabby blends. And their poise, too — their mien. Feral life is not easy. No soft beds and sofas to lounge on, no warm laps on which to lie. Still, they groom themselves and one another, and move with confidence and ease, a certain inner power, an integrity. These are not abused animals that cower and peer up at you with sad eyes.

The next thing that struck me was the distinct, complex, and fully formed personality of each cat. Even today, so many years later, I marvel at these living, breathing miracles of life. I feel that being with these cats was as close as I'll ever get to the Source of life. When I was in their presence, I often felt just a whisper away from the spark that animated these remarkable beings.

I found it difficult to fathom that buried in cats' history lies a chapter that speaks to their near annihilation in medieval Europe. However, with the Australian government's 2015 announcement of plans to slaughter two million feral cats, perhaps history truly does repeat itself. (To be fair, Australia's situation is complex. Feral cats have been blamed for the extinction of several species unique to that country.)

Ironically the qualities that had given cats their royal stature in many countries were what, in Europe during the Middle Ages, became evidence for why they should be destroyed. Originally admired for their aloofness and independence, their skill at catching rodents while prowling at night, their keen eyesight, and their secrecy, cats were made suspect by these very traits during the time of the Inquisition.

The Inquisition's initial purpose was to bring heretical or pagan offshoots, such as the Cathars and Waldensians, back into the fold of the Catholic Church. Then plans changed, and the papacy determined that these religious groups should be destroyed instead. When a soldier of the Albigensian Crusade against the Cathars asked the papal representative how he should tell the difference between the true Catholics and the heretics, the representative supposedly replied, "Caedite eos. Novit enim Dominus qui sunt eius" (which can be loosely translated as "Kill them all, for God knows his own").

Unfortunately for cats, these heretical groups had great respect for felines and associated closely with them. Some, having their origins in ancient Egypt, may have even worshipped them. This information spread during the time of the Episcopal Inquisition in the twelfth century, putting cats directly in the crosshairs.

A cat's place in society was now gauged by the doctrine of the Catholic Church. With respect to cats' aloofness and independence, the church cited Genesis, wherein after creating male and female in his own image, God said, "Be fruitful and multiply, and fill the earth and subdue it, and have dominion over the fish of the sea and over the birds of the sky and over every living thing that moves upon the earth." Animals were created by God to serve and be ruled by humans. If they could not be subdued, there was no place for them in society. Cats, as independent creatures, didn't fit here.

A cat's ability to catch rodents after dark also attracted scrutiny, for two reasons. First, cats were active at night, when all God-fearing beasts should be sleeping. And second, as noted by fifteenth-century printer William Caxton, "The devyl playeth ofte with the synnar, lyke as the catte doth with the mous" — cats catch mice just as the devil catches sinners.

It should come as no surprise that when medieval Europeans considered cats' eyes, rather than marveling at the tapetum lucidum, the layer of tissue lying behind the retina that gives cats their night vision, questions arose as to why their eyes glowed at night like a demon's. The hairs at the tips of their tails now became known as "devil's hairs." And otherworldly screams and howls in the middle of the night most certainly didn't help their cause.

Eventually I became a fixture out back, tucked into the thick undergrowth as one of the colony. From my vantage point, I could spy both entryways leading from the street into our backyard — a narrow sidewalk to the north and a small dirt path to the south. It was along these routes that predators lurked. At night, neighboring dogs would alert me to the approach of deadly-silent coyotes. Packs of raccoons were easier to spot, their lumbering bodies bustling noisily, unable to stifle the eerie high trills of excitement spilling from their mouths in anticipation of a kill.

Both groups of predators concerned me, but historically raccoons were worse in terms of total body count. Working as a team, a half dozen would launch coordinated attacks from both sides of the house, boxing prey into the middle of the yard, then leaping into trees and pounding branches for any cat that sought refuge there. Occasionally they would startle a nesting opossum and its family, and we'd hear hideous screams as they, too, would meet a horrid fate.

I kept an eye trained on the edges of our house; both the north and south paths. There I would occasionally spot a coyote, half its face exposed, one eye scoping out my colony while the rest of its body lurked behind the stucco wall. If they'd come this far into town, they were hungry and willing to take risks. Since we always cleared away any food remaining after we fed the cats, the coyotes weren't there for kibbles. They were there for flesh.

When I would spot a coyote along the north path, I had to keep my eyes on the south. Sometimes another coyote would be hiding there, too. And more than one predator meant double trouble.

I would wait to see if any cat in the colony caught their scent or otherwise became aware of them. Often they did not. When I sensed the coyotes were ready to attack, I would stand up, making my body as large as possible, raising my arms and sticking out my chest, swinging a large stick I carried. Ready to grab the power hose, too, if necessary. The coyotes' eyes would invariably double in size before the stunned creatures charged away. I wanted predators to know that things had changed for good. No more free meals.

Raccoons I had to be more proactive about. Their assaults were more dynamic and calculated, based on power and speed. They could be as dangerous to humans as to cats, so at the first sound of their high trills, I would scare the colony into hiding, then run along the fence, pounding wooden slats with my stick, disrupting the attack, while always planning an escape route for myself in case they came after me.

Of course my interventions terrified the colony, too, causing cats to scatter in fear. But I learned nature is incredibly resilient. When the perceived threat was gone, the colony would reconvene in minutes, almost as though nothing at all had happened. Remaining in stress and hyperventilating, with hormones shooting through their system, saps a tremendous amount of a cat's energy. I marveled at how quickly they regulated themselves once things were safe.

It reminded me of the character Chili Palmer in the movie *Get Shorty* after he nearly died on the balcony.

His lady friend asks, "Were you scared up there?"

He answers, "You bet."

She adds, "You don't act like it."

And he says, "I was scared then, not now. How long you want me to be scared?"

I admit, spotting coyotes ogling my cats, I lost my ability to remain unbiased. We'd lost many fine felines to their hungry jaws, and I was unforgiving. I rationalized that it was stupid to pass judgment on nature, whether it was the hunter and its prey, or an earthquake or tornado, or any other force of nature over which I had no control. But that was my mind talking; my heart was still disturbed.

I had felt the same disturbance around the wild dogs of Nepal. Routinely, once evening and its accompanying cold, thick fog descended over the Kathmandu Valley, packs of canines would appropriate villages as their own. These weren't your tail-wagging, spinning-in-circles, happy-to-see-you pets. These were bloodthirsty, feral half wolves that ran roughshod through the countryside like roided street fighters. Deadly, and to be avoided.

Late at night, hours after taxis had stopped running, on foot and miles from home, as I often found myself, I would encounter these beasts more often than not. Fog-shrouded, dark, crooked lanes and small alleyways were difficult enough to traverse under normal circumstances. Even more so when a roaming pack of feral dogs had picked up your scent.

My first experience with them was while walking with a friend. We had heard their vicious growls, first in the distance, then louder as the dogs approached. But soon they went silent, and my friend and I breathed in relief, confident they had moved on.

Instead, they were poised to attack. The only hint we had that we were about to be mincemeat was the sound of the lead dog's nails scraping the dirt as he ran full speed at us, his minions right behind, like a speeding car with its headlights turned off, heading for a collision. My friend happened to be standing ahead of me and took the full brunt of the attack. They were on him like silent samurais. Flailing to protect himself, he inadvertently kicked the alpha male in the snout, and the dog retreated in yelps — followed, fortunately, by the rest of the pack. My friend had received nasty bites and ended up in the hospital.

How did villagers handle the situation? I decided to follow behind them and find out. Once howls were heard in the distance, they began picking up rocks from the path and tucked them into their shirts. Then as these wild dogs closed in around them, they would hurl the rocks as hard as possible, primarily aiming for the lead dog in order to defuse the attack. They were remarkably accurate shots, as evidenced by alpha males seen in the light of day sporting injured eyes and welts on their foreheads.

I didn't want to throw rocks at dogs but had an idea I thought might work. I experimented the next time I found myself out at night far from home and heard packs of dogs coming my way. I piled rocks into my shirt and waited for them. When their growls went silent and an attack was imminent, I merely shook the rocks in my shirt, alerting the dogs I was locked and loaded, and that's all it took. They begged off rather than risk another stoning.

On the other hand, at the pilgrimage site where I lived, these feral canines were venerated. To understand why, one must first appreciate the dynamic around holy places of Asia. It's an accepted belief there that deities and saints at times disguise themselves at such places to test the devout. So pilgrims tend to treat lepers, beggars, and animals the same way they might a saintly looking monk or nun. Since one can't really tell whom one is dealing with, better to treat all sentient life with reverence. But it goes beyond that. The Divine is present in all living things, even dogs, and so all life is to be respected and honored.

Nepal, being primarily Hindu, specially honors dogs during the five-day autumn festival of Tihar. The Nepali version of Diwali, the ancient Festival of Lights celebrated in India and other Hindu nations throughout Southeast Asia, Tihar is arguably the most important holiday of the year. At its deepest, this is a celebration of light over darkness, knowledge over ignorance, good over evil, and hope over despair. During this time, Hindus venerate not only the deities of their pantheon, but also the animals with whom the celebrants coexist.

Entire days are devoted to crows, cows, and oxen. And on the second day of the festival dogs are honored with garlands, vermilion marks on the forehead, and special meals. Dogs have a noble history in Hindu lore, as guardians of heaven and hell and helpers of Indra, ruler of the heavens. Even the righteous King Yudhishthira, in the epic known as the Mahabharata, refused Indra's request that he leave his dog behind before entering heaven. The story goes something like this:

Indra told Yudhishthira, "All cannot attain heaven. The dog is old and thin and has no value."

"In that case, I do not want to go to heaven," Yudhishthira replied. "The dog was my faithful companion on earth, and the pleasures of heaven mean nothing compared to the grief of losing my beloved companion."

Becoming more emotional, Yudhishthira continued, "He has done nothing to deserve abandonment. If he does not deserve to go to heaven, then neither do I."

"Stop!" Indra cried. "No one has qualities like you, Yudhishthira! You have passed the moral test of life."

Dogs also have a place in the lore of Tibetan Buddhism not dissimilar to that of Yudhishthira and his dog. The spiritual master Kukkuripa cared for a female dog he found starving in the bushes, and he nursed her back to health. The two stayed together in a cave for twelve years while Kukkuripa practiced meditative austerity. His spiritual accomplishments caught the attention of celestial maidens, who invited him to ascend and enjoy all the pleasures of heavenly life. He accepted, but while there, he couldn't stop thinking about his dog. Peering from the heavens, he saw her hungry and sad. Despite the maidens' plea that he stay, he chose to return to his cave and be reunited with his dog. Both were elated upon his return, and when Kukkuripa scratched his dog in joy, suddenly the animal vanished and in her place stood a goddess. She congratulated him on forgoing heaven for a dog and explained that there were greater things than the pleasures of the heavenly realms. She instructed him in releasing the last cords of bondage so that he attained complete enlightenment.

So it was no surprise that when city workers came to my village (where many Tibetan Buddhists resided) to kill packs of feral dogs with poison, residents took it upon themselves to tiptoe behind the executioners and flush poison from the dogs' mouths as soon as it was administered to them. They weren't successful in every case, but they saved many lives that day. One of the survivors was elevated to canine mascot of the village. He had thick golden fur, albeit mangy, as one might expect of a stray dog. The poison affected his central nervous system so that when he walked, he appeared drunk, limbs flailing, unable to amble in a straight line. Still, he was treated like a king. He was given soft pillows to sleep on at night and fed the best food residents of the village could afford.

As I reflected on that unlikely mascot of our village, my thoughts were suddenly shattered by a prehistoric-sounding, piercing screech and rhythmic swooshes of large wings cutting through the night air. I never actually saw this creature, other than as an imposing shadow, though it made its appearance every two weeks or so. It was an enigma in the neighborhood. At the first sound of its call, neighbors would run from their homes, trying to catch sight of it. From what I can tell, nobody ever did, and it was elevated to the status of myth. But with every other wild thing showing up in my backyard, if someone had told me it was a pterodactyl, I wouldn't have blinked an eye.

The colony and I settled back into our familiar positions, as we whiled away countless evening hours together in the jungle enclosure of our yard. I gained an appreciation for small, seemingly insignificant things when watching a rag they dragged from the trash become a throne to lounge on; a broken twig put to shame any toy a pet store might sell.

Weeks and months passed. My rhythm fell in with theirs. I

could tell with a glance whether a cat was ill and whether the problem needed immediate attention or would resolve itself. Other than the occasional threat, which became less frequent the more I stayed with them, the nights were mostly silent. Except for occasional loud squawks from exotic birds I had in fact seen: wild parrots. Often roosting in our trees with their brilliant, variegated shades of green and piercing red eyes, they seemed completely out of place, like a slice of rain forest in a concrete jungle.

How feral parrots came to make Southern California their home is something of a mystery. According to local legend, many were set free to escape the 1959 fire at Simpson's Bird Farm in the San Gabriel Valley. Others may have originated from the Busch Gardens bird sanctuary in Van Nuys when it closed in 1979. Still others were likely let go by smugglers trying to avoid arrest. The Bel Air fire of 1961 was also a likely source, since many residents kept exotic birds and both they and firefighters were said to have released the birds to keep them safe.

I found it ironic that so much wildlife makes its home in the second most populous city in the country. Disparate worlds seemed to cross paths in the vortex of my backyard, an intersection of domesticity and wildness, the tamed and untamed. The ferals certainly touched an untamed place inside me that perhaps lurks inside all of us. I believe it helps define who we are, whether or not we acknowledge its existence. And I found something reassuring in the fact that wildness expressed itself so fully in a densely populated suburb just ten miles from downtown LA. Here the primal had somehow pierced the Lysol veil, inadvertently spoiling the well-laid plans of suburban sensibilities that aspire to cleanliness and predictability, designed to ensure not only that our environment is sterilized, but that our emotions will follow suit.

Yet nature indicates that aspiring to homogenization carries inherent risk. Purebred animals seem to suffer more from genetic disorders than mixed breeds. Monocultures, while perhaps efficient, are not particularly resilient — as proved by the potato famine of nineteenth-century Ireland, the corn blight of the 1970s, and even the challenges facing the popular Cavendish bananas of today. Genetic uniformity weakens crops to the degree that they are decimated when attacked by pathogens. In every case, remedies have been discovered only when scientists have sought out wild varieties of those agricultural products. It is in wildness that strength and resilience are found and balance restored.

While neighborhoods may maintain the appearance of neat and clean, it's what goes on inside each home that matters. Keeping the yard mowed is one thing; restraining the primal brain is something else altogether. Especially when it receives copious nourishment from the television shows, movies, and other media that most people feed it daily. It's the oldest part of the brain and the one most easily triggered when survival is at stake. Fight or flight, might is right, me against them. The reptilian brain is territorial. Feral. Still, we act shocked when someone can no longer keep it under wraps and the wild animal gets loose, making for the violent and highly disturbing news items that appear daily.

Negative influences seem to have a deeper impact on the human psyche than positive ones. The trauma of negative experiences can last a lifetime, but the elation of joyous ones rarely does. This is reflected even in language. Two-thirds of all words in the English language pertaining to emotions are negative. And of the words that describe personality traits, three-fourths are negative. This skewed ratio can affect human relationships profoundly. John Gottman, a world-renowned expert on relationships and marriage, has determined that in the context of relationships, positive interactions must outnumber negative ones by no less than five to one. If the ratio drops below that, the relationship is unlikely to last.

While the brain might be the trigger, the wellspring of primal emotions resides in the lower abdomen. Which is why most people breathe only into the upper chest, shallowly, where it's safe. Breathing deep into the belly, diaphragmatically, while keeping the upper chest still, puts one in touch with that hidden primal pool, the often unconscious driving force behind our actions. It is here that people can discover why they sabotage themselves despite their own best efforts. Or that the life they are living has not been by choice, but by compromise. Here they can recognize their deepest fears as unsubstantiated, those unnamed vague terrors that have been driving them all this time seen as nothing more than imagination. Though perhaps scary, breathing into the deep recesses of one's being can also be revelatory. The lower abdomen — known as the *hara* (Japanese) or *dantian* (Chinese) in the Eastern traditions of martial arts, acupuncture, and chi kung — is the body's true center of power.

As the Gospel of Thomas tells us, "If you bring forth what is within you, what you bring forth will save you. If you do not bring forth what is within you, what you do not bring forth will destroy you."

I grew up in a house where wild things were killed with regularity. Monthly exterminator visits made sure of that. I wasn't well prepared, then, for what I found when I moved to Nepal. For a time, I lived with a Tibetan family from Shigatse. The wife's brother owned a small noodle shop along the main trade route linking Nepal with Tibet, where he served mostly a traditional Tibetan soup called *thukpa*.

We ate so much thukpa, the running joke was "Thukpa mambo tuna kukpa chagi re," meaning "If you eat a lot of thukpa, you're gonna go mad." The Tibetans loved when I visited the noodle shop, because prior to arriving in Nepal, I had been taught the language, albeit in its archaic form — the equivalent, perhaps, of Elizabethan English. I became the laughingstock of the place, the court jester. Anything I said in Tibetan was met with howls of laughter, tears streaming down faces, and yells begging me to "Say it again! Say it again!"

The first time I entered the noodle shop, it took my eyes a while to adjust to its cave-like darkness. Finally making out four small tables, I sat down at one of them. As the rest of my surroundings came into focus, I noticed the wall facing me undulating with movement. I couldn't tell what was causing the motion until I looked closer and realized the entire wall was covered with huge cockroaches. Floor to ceiling and from one end of the wall to the other.

I must've missed the board-of-health letter grades outside. In that moment, it truly sunk in that I wasn't in Kansas anymore. I remember being so overwhelmed that I actually had no response. Then, regaining my senses, I thought to run — until I considered that for all I knew, this was the Spago of noodle shops and anywhere else I might go to eat could be worse. Hard to imagine but still a possibility. My only solace was in knowing there weren't any ghosts inside. I found out that the three-foot-high doorway I had stooped through to enter the noodle shop made sure of this, since, according to custom, ghosts cannot bend at the waist.

I heard a rustling in the bushes and glanced over at the cats for their reaction. They didn't seem concerned. I stood up quietly anyhow, listening closely. Then I spotted a long white nose and dark beady eyes and breathed in relief. It was just an opossum. The cats spent countless hours marveling at these creatures that made their home in the trees. The opossums' terrible eyesight ensured the cats could safely get an up-close view of their prehistoric claws, each pink digit and sharp nail wrapping itself around the fence as they deliberately inched along, foraging for food.

They would navigate with their noses, their sense of smell

allegedly more dependable than their eyesight. But I wasn't convinced. Often a foraging opossum would run smack into a group of cats resting on their haunches, then leap in the air surprised, proving that both their eyesight and their sense of smell had failed them. I considered opossums comic relief (like the plentiful skunks in the area, especially the babies — you have no idea how cute). Our indoor cats did, too. They would run to the backdoor screen and climb over one another to get a better view of these strange creatures. Under the right circumstances, however, opossums could be vicious, with a mouthful of sharp teeth.

Years later, we rescued three feral-kitten sisters from the colony and brought them inside to safety, to live with us. Every day, we took them outside on body leashes for fresh air and exercise, and often spotted an animated opossum couple that lived nearby. Always in a hurry like the White Rabbit in *Alice in Wonderland*, the couple would tear around the corner of the house, shoulder to shoulder, smacking into each other like bumper cars, not caring what they ran into, whether it was a cat or a tree stump or a sprinkler head. They would even run into me, too, if I didn't move. I called it "running by braille."

One of the kitten sisters, a lovely white tabby, had never before seen a creature like this in her short life. We watched as the bumper-car opossum couple came tearing around the corner. Just inches from the bewildered tabby now, one of them reached out and snapped its jaws at her as it passed, startling us both. After about a minute of thinking about it, when the kitten realized what had happened, she hissed and growled back, surprising even herself, I think. Note to self: I must teach her about timing.

I was comfortable in the backyard among wild things. It reminded me that I usually felt comfortable in the wild. During my first winter in Nepal studying pilgrimage sites, I arrived at a Himalayan monastery during a driving snowstorm. Given the significance of this location, I figured I'd need at least a week there to complete my research. I asked the head lama if I might possibly stay. He apologized for the monastery being so small, admitting that all the rooms were occupied. But he did offer me the choice of sharing rooms with one of two people.

The first was a simple monk, very serene, quiet, and contemplative. The other was a Golok warrior from the furthest reaches of Tibet bordering Mongolia. I peered into his room and saw a shirtless, crazy-looking man spinning a prayer wheel and fingering a rosary, sitting in piles of snow that had accumulated through the room's broken windows. For him it seemed a balmy summer day. He gave me a look right out of *One Flew over the Cuckoo's Nest.*

The lama pulled me aside, warning that Goloks could be violent and ferocious. The name *Golok* itself implies decapitation (*go,* "head"; *lok,* "lop off"). He wanted to be absolutely sure I understood that should we quarrel for some reason, I would likely be killed.

Of course I chose the Golok.

Beneath this monastery, in the deep underbrush along the river below, lies a haunting temple where animal sacrifices are made to a wrathful female goddess statue on Tuesday and Saturday each week. When you walk the path toward that temple, the temperature turns chill, as if warning that all but the strong of heart should turn away. Death soaks the air. On the days of animal sacrifices, the monks on top of the hill do extra rituals for the souls of animals that have lost their lives there.

About sixty miles northeast of there, another pilgrimage site honors a much different type of sacrifice. One arrives there by trekking through small villages where fruit bats dart by with high-pitched screams and plungers thump, piston-like, in long wooden cylinders used for making yak-butter tea. Mothers call out to their young even though they play at their feet. A reassuring banter meaning "I'm here. Are you there?" And the children's reply,

"Yes, I'm here. Are you?" Like the chirping of birds, these calls between mother and child continue as one approaches a pristine Himalayan foothill valley. Engulfed in flapping, colorful prayer flags, this is the place where the Buddha in a previous life offered his body to a starving tigress, so that she could feed her hungry cubs. It is called Takmo Lujin (from *tak*, "tiger"; *mo*, "female"; *lu*, "holy body"; and *jin*, "offered").

As for my time with the Golok, things couldn't have gone more smoothly. He never slept, and since I didn't know what I was up against, my sleep was intermittent at best. Not to mention the fact that without windowpanes, there was no barrier to the bitter cold or the snowdrifts piling up around us. For all I knew, he had broken the windows himself just to get some ventilation in the place.

Windblown and sporting a Dalai Lama pin stuck right through the skin of his ruddy chest, with the click of his rosary beads measuring time like a clock's second hand, the Golok stared at me, day and night. Anytime I happened to look over, there were his sparkling eyes staring back, twinkling, piercing, looking right through me, his wild look impossible to decipher.

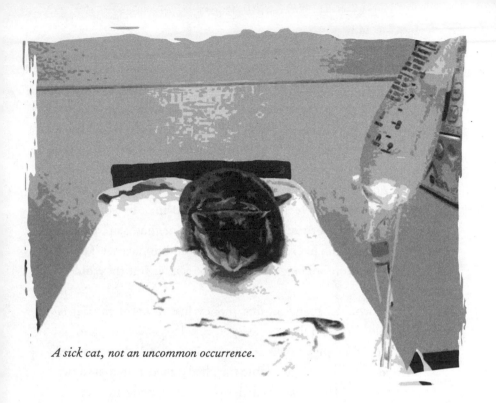

A sick cat, not an uncommon occurrence.

7 Dr. V, Miracle Worker

O nce we accepted responsibility for the cats, we knew that sooner or later we would need the services of a vet. Ah, vets. Finding a good one is tough, truth be told. All it takes is a quick scan through Yelp reviews of vets throughout the country to see how many problematic places exist.

According to many reviews, either the medical service is inferior or there's price gouging. Inferior medical service is perhaps the more subjective of the two. I cut vets a lot of slack in that area unless there is gross negligence, given how challenging it must be to treat patients who can't tell you what's wrong, where they're feeling pain, or what they ate, drank, or swallowed.

Price gouging, on the other hand, disturbs me, as it usually occurs when the pet owner is most vulnerable, with a severely sick or injured pet.

Once, before we found our "miracle vet" (yes, we really did find one), one of our cats had symptoms that could have indicated one of three diseases, two of which were 100 percent fatal. I took the cat to several vets who quoted me north of five thousand dollars for the proper tests and who, on top of that, said exploratory surgery would likely be needed, at an additional cost. I truly thought they were joking, and started to smile. But they didn't smile back.

"Why would I spend all that money just to know my cat is going to die?" I asked them.

"We just thought you would want to know" was their answer.

Wondering how many people they had duped with that logic, I said snarkily, "Here's an idea: How about treating the cat for the one disease with these symptoms that isn't lethal, and if they recover, fine. If not, the cat was going to die anyway, right?"

One vet reluctantly agreed, and I was out the door for $150. Turns out the cat did survive, as did my bankroll.

No, we needed a special vet. One sensitive to our plight and who would not be averse to working with ferals. And hopefully one who would work within our budget, or lack thereof, allowing us to make monthly payments for more expensive procedures, should they arise — and we knew they would. We scoured the internet for reviews of local vets, and it seemed hit-or-miss. Besides exorbitant prices, the other major complaint was lack of bedside manner. The expensive ones are self-explanatory. The bedside manner issue is more personal — you just don't feel the vet truly understands you or your pet.

The vets with the highest ratings in our neighborhood were booked solid. But I did find one whom I thought might fit the bill. His reviews were extremely mixed. People either loved or loathed him. The reviewers who had issues with him shared the same complaint: if he didn't like you, he gave you and your pet poor service. But the raves said that if he liked you, you were golden. This was my guy.

I set up an appointment to meet the vet, explaining to the receptionist, Stacey, that I didn't have a pet in distress but just wanted to have a chat with the doctor. The clinic itself was somewhat run-down, but inviting and very clean inside. The facility as a whole was quite large, with a surgical wing and an area for ailing pets staying longer-term. I have to admit, though, the two-story surgery wing, looming behind the main building, tucked among gnarled trees, with its small, barred Gothic-seeming windows, looked like Frankenstein's lab. It creeped me out every time. I don't know why.

I was led down the hallway to Dr. V's office. He wasn't there, so I sat across from his imposing desk. The room was decorated like the tropics. A fan was blowing, rustling his exuberant plants. On the wall hung colorful paintings of palm trees and beaches, and several votive candles were lit on his desk.

A multitude of framed pictures situated on his desk with their backs to me indicated a large extended family. The diplomas on the wall indicated he had been educated in Southeast Asia, and by their date, I guessed he was now around sixty years of age. He entered the room with a rousing hello, and we shook hands. He asked me to take a seat and then sat at his desk. He scanned the room as if seeing it for the first time, briefly making eye contact with me several times. I could tell he was checking out my vibe, more than anything he could determine by actually looking at me.

I asked about his family and if they were well, how often he returned to his homeland, and whether he had plans to return again soon. He replied that he tried to get there twice a year. I mentioned that his family there must be very proud of him for his great success and reputation here, and he smiled broadly. He asked about my parents and if they were happy, and I said they were. He wanted to know about my siblings and whether I was married and had children. I told him I had never married or had children, as I hadn't met a person I thought I could love for a lifetime. I left that open to interpretation: whether it meant I was incapable of loving someone for a lifetime or I hadn't found something that lovable.

We never spoke one word about pets. Not a breath. After some time, we both fell quiet and watched the trees swaying outside through the window for a while. He glanced at me again, perhaps seeing if I was getting impatient. Then he smiled and rose from his chair, and I followed his lead. We shook hands, and as he led me from the room, he gave me a wink. I knew I was in.

And with no time to spare. As mentioned earlier, a beautiful and rare solid-white kitten from the colony (one of only two pure whites we'd see in twenty years) choked to death on a chicken bone from a neighbor's trash. I later learned that had I been able to catch her and get her to a vet in time, she might have been saved — there is an implement that slides down the throat, turns, and lifts up, dislodging anything stuck in the throat. But in this case, the kitten was dead before I could even put on my shoes and go outside to examine her.

Whenever a cat died in my care, I felt powerless, overwhelmed by grief, and a failure for not protecting the cats as I had promised, and I sought solace wherever I could find it. Sometimes I remembered the oft-told story of the Buddha and the mustard seed: A woman named Kisa Gotami lost her only child. Mad with grief, she carried the dead child in her arms, looking for anyone who might be able to provide medicine to cure her child. A neighbor suggested she visit the Buddha. The Buddha told her to gather a mustard seed from a house that had not known death and he would prepare medicine for the child. She went from door to door, and though everyone was willing to give her the mustard seed, no house had been untouched by death. Realizing the impermanence of life and feeling empathy for others who had also lost loved ones, she went and buried her child.

When that story didn't help, I contemplated a phrase I had once heard: "crying at a birth and rejoicing at a funeral." Though people delight in new life, just as we did when a new batch of kittens would be presented to us by proud feline mothers, it's a soul entering an uncertain world with no guarantees. Pain is certain to follow; it's just a matter of how soon and to what degree. But when death comes, there is the sense of the soul being released, of returning to the Source. Somehow that seemed right and brought me solace. In my darkest hours, any comfort was welcome.

The tragedy of the white cat choking to death was the catalyst for my determining to regulate the colony's diet. Besides the risks inherent in scavenging for food, it was obvious by looking at their coats that these cats weren't receiving proper nourishment. As clueless as a new dad looking through rows of Gerber's baby food, I perused the myriad choices of cat food stacked floor to ceiling at a nearby PetSmart.

I stood next to an elderly Latina dressed like she had just left church, even though it was a Tuesday. Her cart was filled with everything cat. Canned food, dry food, toys, and small, tasty treats, which I would later learn were basically crack cocaine for cats — except healthy. She examined a pile of coupons in her hand as she compared labels of cans on the shelf. What struck me most was how unhappy she seemed. She attempted a smile my way but failed.

I mentioned that it looked like she had a lot of cats. She shook her head no — they weren't hers. But they depended on her. She was all alone, she explained, and so began feeding neighborhood strays. Having no family or friends, she found purpose in caring for these cats. Uh-oh, I thought, the stereotypical cat lady. And already her story was sounding uncomfortably close to mine. I decided that when I began going out in my Sunday best on Tuesdays I would worry, but not until then.

She continued her story. It seemed her neighbors had been friendly to her before she began caring for these cats. Now these same neighbors made a point of killing one cat a week and leaving its filleted body in her driveway. And to add to her worries, she was on welfare and her subsidies were being cut — meaning she didn't know how she was going to cover her own expenses, let alone continue to care for the cats, and would probably need to move, putting the cats that remained behind at risk.

I asked whether she was sure they were strays and not feral. This is an important distinction to make. Stray cats are domestic, and so can be resocialized. They knew human contact prior to running away, getting lost, or being abandoned. Ferals, on the other hand, are wild and remain antisocial. Strays tend to be disheveled and dirty, while ferals are generally clean and well groomed. Strays travel alone; ferals move with a colony. Strays tend to approach people, homes, or cars. Ferals avoid such contact. Strays will make eye contact and be vocal, might beg, and may be seen during the day. Ferals avoid people and will not beg. They rarely make eye contact or purr or meow, and they tend to avoid the daylight.

She felt that her cats were stray, she explained, since they would come right up to her, rub against her, and let her hold them. Yep, I thought, those are strays. If I were to try that with my cats, I'd be shredded wheat. I suggested she take them to a no-kill animal shelter where they could then be adopted out. That way she would know they were safe and would no longer have problems with her neighbors.

I don't think she heard a word I said. Sometimes one's troubles can seem so overwhelming that there's no space to take in any more. As I studied her worried face, I also surreptitiously studied her cart. Specifically I was seeing what type of dry cat food she was buying. I bought the same.

Not three days later did Tiny become severely constipated. By the fourth day, she couldn't pass anything at all. Dammit, the curse of the stray-cat lady! In acute cases, a constipated cat needs to be seen by a vet immediately, as toxins backed up in the system can quickly kill them. So here was my first experience with Dr. V as healer.

I called his office and was told to bring Tiny in *stat*. Dr. V maintained his same easygoing manner, even in crisis — or rather, what I considered a crisis. He had the attitude of a medic having survived both world wars and having treated every cat injury imaginable. Stories you'd never want to hear. Putting kitty-cat heads back on, replacing tails, fusing limbs, prosthetics, shrapnel wounds. Nothing could faze him.

He gently felt Tiny's belly and couldn't affect her condition through massage. She was too impacted, he said. He glanced my way and said she'd need to stay overnight, then left the room. I hurried to Stacey at the reception desk, wondering what that meant.

"Oh, he's probably going to give her a series of enemas to unclog her, and he wants to keep her overnight to make sure she's clear."

"Overnight?"

"Overnight," she giggled.

What did that giggle mean? And isn't anything overnight expensive? Hotels tend to be expensive. Next-day mail delivery ain't cheap. Hospital stays have pricey written all over them.

"How much is an overnight gonna set me back?" I casually asked, as if price were no object.

That giggle again. A giggle like she's part of a serious profit-sharing plan.

"We'll see how the doctor decides to bill it," she answered.

I wondered what that meant. Same ballpark as what a plumber decides to bill for a Sunday night emergency? And speaking of plumbers, I wondered how much enemas cost. Did they offer a cheap version? Did I have any input here?

I returned the next day to pick up Tiny. Dr. V was nowhere to be seen, but Tiny seemed in good spirits, and her chirping mews meant she was happy to see me. I tried to sense from her what staying in Frankenstein's lab all night had been like and whether Igor had treated her well. And then came the bill. That giggle again from Stacey as she pored over the three-page bill. Three pages? For one overnight? Maybe he doodles a lot or adds cartoons, I thought. Ah, this must be one page in triplicate.

"Wow, three pages," Stacey said to herself out loud.

I think I had turned pale, because Stacey asked if I wanted to sit down.

"Well," she finally said. "He must really like you. Have a look at this."

And there was the bill in all its glory. Names of procedures and medicines I had never heard of, and the prices next to them like those of exotic types of caviar air-freighted from Moscow at my expense. And at the very bottom, tucked beneath many large numbers and decimal points was a very strange word: *discount*. And that discount was 70 percent of the bill. My eyes widened at Stacey.

"I know!" she said.

All I can say is thank goodness for discounts, because over the next week, I had four more cats equally constipated, and each needed an overnight stay with the same protocol. And dear Dr. V gave me the same discount every time.

On my fourth visit, Dr. V just stared at me and asked, "Are you sure you're not a lawyer?"

I assured him that I was not. He continued, certain that I was. I kept looking for the smile, but it wasn't forthcoming.

Finally he said, "I'm sure you're a lawyer because every cat you bring in here is full of shit."

Then came the laugh. I assured him that had I been a lawyer, I wouldn't have needed the discounts he so generously offered. I thanked him from the bottom of my heart, which he accepted graciously, aware that his generosity meant everything to me. It made the difference between a cat living or dying, as far as I was concerned.

Since Dr. V and Stacey seemed merged at the hip, I felt comfortable speaking with Stacey about anything I might speak to the doctor about. I wanted to know why my cats were all having digestive distress. She asked for the brand name of the dry food I was feeding them, and then nodded with a smile.

"When you get home," she said, "have a look at the ingredients. First ingredient is probably cornmeal. Any cat food with a grain as its primary ingredient is going to clog up your cat. They're carnivores; they don't need carbs. Anything besides protein is filler."

She went on to explain that ingredients sometimes posing as natural or healthy alternatives for cats can actually be dangerous to them. Even animal proteins can vary a lot, she said; chicken by-products, for instance (you don't want to know), instead of chicken breasts or thighs. Then she told me they weigh the protein before it is dehydrated, so I should make sure animal proteins make up a large percentage of the overall content of the food.

Once I switched to the brand Stacey recommended (Purina ONE), which besides high-quality proteins also contained three varieties of fish oils, we never again had another case of blocked colons. Purina ONE was more expensive than the bargain basement brand I previously purchased, but well worth it. The cats were no longer in distress. And in a short amount of time, a luster I'd never seen before appeared on their coats. At last they were receiving proper nourishment.

Snow White, her daughter Caliby, and her son Jaguar.

8 Supporting My New Family

O nce I had committed to the colony — though I never spoke it aloud — I knew I would do anything for those cats. Even humiliate myself, which is what ended up happening. I knew a little something about astrology, enough to be dangerous. A passing remark in the late 1990s to a friend over lunch, that based on the planetary alignment at that time, I felt the NASDAQ index had peaked and investors should probably liquidate their positions or short the market (a technique of making money on stocks that are falling) had somehow leaked through the grapevine. My comment happened to fall on the ears of a Hollywood money manager. Soon my phone was ringing. People of prominence were on the other end wanting my advice. I tried to turn them down, admitting I was a hack, but they took that as modesty. Little did they know.

But the cats had to eat, so read for them I did. Suddenly I had access. It was the magical key that bridged the previously restricted threshold to Hollywood's elite. I couldn't do it as a hack screenwriter but could as a hack astrologer. This turn of events was so stereotypical Hollywood it almost made me gag.

Besides individual readings, I was even hired to read astrology charts at Hollywood parties. At the parties I'd attended until then, the only way you'd see stars is if you got punched in the face. Now it was like the Milky Way. Once, the hosts even made me wear a turban. In the middle of reading for an aspiring actor who would later go on to win an Oscar, one seductive starlet who had been lying on the bed watching me reached out and pulled me onto the bed with her, wrapping her legs around me, not letting go. But would anyone read my screenplays? No.

Still, it got me a private audience in a high-rise luxury film-production suite overlooking the Pacific Ocean with an Oscar-winning producer. For some reason, the chart indicated this man would have some type of mouth issue. Could it be problems with the teeth? Jaw? No, Mars was the influence here, so something related to blood. Gums maybe? He denied everything.

Ah, at last my cover had been blown. Thank goodness. Just as I readied to slink from the room apologetically, I happened to notice small streaks of blood trickling from his mouth that he would wipe occasionally with white Kleenex, turning it crimson. I held his gaze.

"What?" he asked.

"Oh nothing."

"What?" he insisted.

"Well, could that be the blood from the mouth I was talking about?"

"No, no, no, this is just an allergy. I've had it forever."

Alrighty then.

After the reading, as we exchanged pleasantries, I mentioned to him that I was working on a fascinating project that I owned the life rights to. Might he be interested in hearing about it?

"Umm, no."

But what did follow was an invitation to a major production company to do a reading for its special effects supervisor. He wondered about only one thing: the viability of a film project the studio had already spent tens of millions of dollars on in preproduction. When he told me the date the partnership deal had been signed, I knew for a fact, just as I had about the NASDAQ crash, this project was doomed.

The day he'd signed that deal was such a horrific day astrologically, it's amazing the sun even rose. I told him to quietly look for another project to fall back on, because I could guarantee, with complete certainty, the project would be delayed. He asked if it was dead, and I said no. I felt it would revive after a year and a half or so but would bring in nowhere near the revenue they expected. I told him to make sure he delegated responsibilities so that he wouldn't take the fall for a weak film.

Turns out, a month later the studio pulled the plug on the project. Taking my advice, he had already segued into another film and quietly brought his team with him. He was elated.

"How can I thank you?" he wondered. "Is there anything I can do for you?"

"Would you mind reading my screenplay?"

"Uh, no."

But a year and a half later (when that original film project did, in fact, get revived), the executive who had followed my advice and put others in charge (who did indeed take the fall for a disappointing box office) put me in contact with the head of a major motion picture studio who felt he could make my script see the light of day. Coming off the biggest hit of his long and storied career, he had carte blanche to make any movie he chose as his next film. He became enamored with my project, and that it was based on a true story made it all the more compelling to him.

That led to a trip to San Francisco to read charts for an employee of George Lucas. Afterward I was invited to Skywalker Ranch in Marin County to watch the final edits on the last *Star Wars* prequel, *Revenge of the Sith*. The facility, tucked amid green rolling hills and trees, truly was remarkable. The main mansion was a veritable museum of George Lucas films, where props and costumes were on display, including the original light sabers from the first *Star Wars* films. The vaulted stained glass window library was also a highlight. I was convinced this was an amazing place to work, as every single person I passed had a smile plastered across their face they couldn't erase.

The following week, I was invited to a private screening of *Revenge of the Sith* for Lucasfilm employees and their families and friends. Later that day, I went to the grand opening of Lucasfilm's new home in the Presidio, by the Golden Gate Bridge. The facility and the exhibitions for the opening were tremendously impressive, as was a sit-down meal with VIPs at every table, a who's who of industry people, including George Lucas himself. Oh, and we were served hors d'oeuvres by robots.

On the drive back to Los Angeles from San Francisco, I realized powerful people in Hollywood didn't appreciate the astrology so much as they appreciated my honesty. I could tell them things no one else dared. I was fearless because I was reading the planets. It wasn't personal. Had I been pitching them my project, I would've been shaking in my boots. But I could stand in complete confidence and tell a Hollywood power broker that he was essentially powerless, as I did once. Their bluster was a cover for a deep lack of confidence, and they were surrounded by yes-men.

Nobody spoke to them this way. I had no horse in the race, so I could call it the way I saw it.

I reflected on my good luck at having finally gotten access and the famous people with whom I had been able to rub shoulders. I dined at restaurants with A-list celebrities and visited them at their homes. I watched *The Tonight Show* from backstage, traipsing into the green room on occasion, calling everyone I could think of, bragging about where I was, while eating grapes from bowls laden with ripe fruit. Bored, I ventured onto another soundstage where a major motion picture was being shot, and returned just in time for the show's end, greeting Jay Leno and bandleader Kevin Eubanks, telling them what a great show it had been. Jay and company accepted the compliment with wry looks on their faces, just dying to ask, "Who are you, and what the hell are you doing here?"

But that glow faded fast when I got real and concluded I was no closer to breaking in than before. I was just a gun for hire. On a temporary visa that could be revoked at any time. My phone could stop ringing tomorrow, which is essentially what happened. A friend told me it was for the best. Hollywood would've destroyed me, he said. "You'd have three ex-wives milking you for all you're worth, a pile of bratty kids, and six ulcers." I guessed he was right, but what a way to go.

Desire is both a strong motivator and a strong ensnarer. One spiritual teacher I met described desire as hunger — chewing on the bone of life, pursuing everything we think will give us satisfaction. But actually the meat from the bone is long gone, and what we're really tasting is our own blood from the shards of bone as they cut into our gums.

I realized I had been living in imagination, building sand

castles in the air, driven by the eight worldly knots: we hope to be praised and are afraid of being criticized; we are looking for fame and are afraid of being disgraced; we want to gain something and are afraid of losing it; we are striving for happiness and are afraid of misery.

I arrived home from San Francisco late that night and couldn't wait to be outside in the bushes with my family, a pile of wild cats. The kind of success I was chasing in the movie business was ephemeral, I reasoned in the thick night air. This was really where I belonged, in the deep underbrush with my companions. Of course, it was an especially easy conclusion to draw, given that I had no other options.

Though the astrology was heady stuff, it was intermittent and didn't cover the bills, and monthly food and vet bills were piling up. Then a virus spread through a handful of feral kittens we had saved, landing them in the hospital with IVs for a week. Let's see, five cats in pet ICU for five days. I guessed I should start prostituting myself that evening. Seriously mulling over that option, I had a flash of a better idea. Trading commodities. Something I had done in years past.

Impossible as it may seem, I'm more a hack commodity trader than a hack screenwriter and astrologer. Trading energy, metals, livestock, meat, and agricultural markets in highly leveraged positions is like walking a tightrope without a net. I'd fallen on my face more times than I cared to remember, eventually realizing I was no better than a degenerate gambler who had self-destructed from consistently making bad bets. I know my brokers still stand around the watercooler reminiscing about the trades I made. Historically awful trades. In fact, I'm convinced that whenever I would place a trade, the entire brokerage firm probably took the opposite position. I was wrong so many times I became a contrary indicator.

Commodity trading is dangerous. The risk of loss can be

substantial. For a relatively small investment, say five thousand dollars, one can leverage a large commodity position, say one hundred thousand dollars. This works out well if you're on the right side of a trade. But if the market turns against you, you must quickly decide whether to cut your losses or hope the market will turn back around. In a fast market, every second, even if you only hold a small position, can be worth thousands of dollars or more. One thousand, two thousand, six months of cat food, what are you going to do? Five thousand, seven thousand, there goes the vet fund for a year...

The worst, or best, scenario, depending on which side of the trade you're on, occurs when a particular commodity market moves its limit for the day — either high or low. This is called a "limit move" or "lock limit." A frost scare in coffee. A drought in grains. A freeze in orange juice. Mad cow disease for meats. These scare events can cause a market to move its daily limit. If you happen to own contracts in those commodities, it is impossible to get out as trading has closed for the day. If it's a severe issue, that market can stay lock limit for days, even weeks. For example, in a volatile market, the market may open for half a second, the limit move takes place, and the market is closed again for the day. No way to get in or out, yet the limit move has occurred anyway. So if corn is locked after its 40 cent limit move, every day that market is moving 40 cents, either with you or against you, depending on what side of the trade you're on. And a 40 cent move in corn is two thousand dollars per contract. You've got ten contracts? You're making or losing twenty thousand dollars a day.

If you're on the wrong side of the trade, you're looking for the first freighter to Alaska. Or for your mortgage papers and car title because you're about to lose both. If you're on the right side of the trade, you're ecstatic. Every day of continuous lock-limit moves is making you money exponentially. Even stop-loss orders, used to automatically get traders out of their positions, can be powerless during limit moves.

Then there's the dreaded early-morning margin call from the brokerage firm. If you don't want Guido and friends over for lunch, you must make a deposit by the end of the day to cover your losses.

But it sure beats prostituting myself, I reasoned. My brokers snickered when I reestablished contact.

"Of course we remember you."

I heard them laughing in the background. Well, that didn't bolster my confidence.

I watched the colony through the screen door as they rubbed each other, knowing it was feeding time. Seeing the empty bags of cat food in front of me, I interrupted the laughter to say I'd be wiring a thousand bucks over that day.

More laughs. "We look forward to it."

Lined up on the fence.

9 The Naming of Cats

L et me preface this chapter by saying it's about doting on cats and not for the faint of heart. If you didn't already think I should be locked in a padded white room, you'll certainly be convinced of it by the end of this chapter.

In his inimitable work *Old Possum's Book of Practical Cats*, which later became the basis for the hit musical *Cats*, poet T.S. Eliot wrote that every cat has three names: one particular, one peculiar, and one dignified. Our cat naming followed a similar course.

I told myself that naming the cats would help me keep track of them. But I was lying. These remarkable creatures brought purpose to my life, and I wanted to name them to honor our relationship. Besides, there seemed a historical precedent for naming animals. Bucephalus, Alexander the Great's favorite horse. Ham the Astrochimp. Toto, Shamu, Lassie. I'll bet even Mrs. O'Leary's cow had a name. Paul Revere's borrowed horse certainly did.

The naming of animals is even mentioned in the Old Testament:

The Lord God said: "It is not good that the man should be alone; I will make him a helper as his partner."

So out of the ground the Lord God formed every animal of the field and every bird of the air, and brought them to the man to see what he would call them; and whatever the man called every living creature would be its name. The man gave names to all cattle, and to the birds of the air, and to every animal of the field.

According to the Kabalistic interpretation of these verses, the names Adam gave the animals were not merely chosen at random, but rather were based on the life-source expression, the Shechinah (Divine Presence), that each creature of God possessed. This is similar to given names in Sanskrit, the liturgical language of ancient India. In Sanskrit, names were intentional, provided by seers who were in communion with the vibration of the object being named. By intoning its given name then, one would actually manifest the thing being addressed, whether material object or divine presence.

Being deaf to nature's vibrational song, as unfortunately most of us are today, doesn't mean the music has ceased playing. Everything on earth vibrates in some fashion, no matter how subtle, even if we're unaware of it. There are even ways to quantify these invisible tones and pulsations. Cymatics, for example, attempts to do this by studying the visible expression of sound in patterns of fine sand or liquid.

Even simpler, ever notice how people with the same name often share similar characteristics? Or perhaps how you immediately like or dislike someone when first hearing their name, even before you know them? It's because the vibration of their name has, to some degree, influenced who they've become. Then imagine how our recurring thoughts have molded us. There may be solid reasoning behind sayings like "You are what you think" and "What you think, you become."

Our naming of cats did not rest on deep insight or on physics. There was no profound meaning behind the process. Usually their color or a personality quirk were the limited inspirations for the names we gave our cats.

While I was glad Adam set a precedent for naming animals, I sensed there was a downside to the tradition he started. A feeling lingered that by naming the cats, we were somehow restricting, pigeonholing, putting a comfortable frame around something wild, spontaneous, and awesome. I didn't want these animals to be our pets or for us to relate to them as such. I wanted to keep the freshness of our relationship, the complete surprise. I didn't want tame animals. I thought of the cat in Neil Gaiman's book *Coraline*, who said, "Now, you people have names. That's because you don't know who you are. We know who we are, so we don't need names."

But the cats having names certainly came in handy during our much-anticipated annual Kitty Oscar Award ceremony, the "Koscars" for short.

Every year, Sophie, Heather, and I voted for Smartest, Most Improved, Best Coat, Prettiest Eyes, Best Mother, Cutest Sleeping Spot, and Best Tail. Five pages' worth of categories. I should add the caveat that not everyone looked forward to the Koscars. Tiny loathed them. We surmised it was because she felt she wouldn't get nominated for anything, which is why she routinely shredded the ballots before anyone could vote.

We purposely added categories she was sure to win, and she reluctantly let things proceed (little did she know those categories included Worst Temper and Meanest to Other Cats). Personally I found it hard to remain unbiased during Koscar season. My housemates teased me mercilessly when Princess, a cat with whom I was enamored because of her regal temperament and having survived a particularly harrowing brush with death, received all my votes, no matter what the category. I couldn't help myself.

T. S. Eliot was right, as many of our cats did sport multiple names. Tiny in particular. Among her names were Teena, Loretta, Mrs. Charnofsky, Pacoima, Hezbollah (when she was a terror), Shredder, and Sophia. She also had numerous songs composed about her.

As did the starlet white tabby we named Cozy and often referred to as Coco Minaj. Here's the first verse of "The Ballad of Coco Minaj":

> She's the prettiest girl west of the Pecos,
> Been known to make grown men cry,
> With her couture dresses and stunning tresses
> Suitors fall to their knees by and by.

The "make grown men cry" line was from an actual event. When she was a kitten, we saved her from certain death at the jaws of predators who'd snatched her littermate the night before. We kept her safe inside, only to have her escape and not return for two days. I was certain she had been killed, and I cried my eyes out for hours on end. The tears were for her, certainly, but they were also from all the pent-up sorrow of having lost so many cats over the years. Anguish I just couldn't keep bottled up inside any longer.

By late morning on the second day of her absence, I was a mess. I went outside in tears, and there, just outside the door, crouched Snow White, Cozy's normally reclusive feral Siamese mother, as if expecting me. We locked eyes, and like an idiot, I pleaded with her to bring her kitten back to me. I'd heard that cats respond better to images than words, so I tried sending her the mental image of her daughter being back inside our house. Later that evening, I heard the strangest noise. I wouldn't characterize it as a cat noise — more of a grunting or snorting. Certainly done on purpose to get my attention, for I have never heard Snow White make another noise like it since. In fact, she has never made a single noise in all the years we've known her. Except for that night.

Looking outside, I saw Snow White, with little Cozy at her feet. Mother stared at me, moving her head down to her kitten, gesturing. I ever so slowly reached down, scooped Cozy up, and brought her into the house.

This was not an isolated event. At least a dozen times since, whenever a cat we cared for escaped or was missing from the colony, we would ask the others for help. Usually within hours, they would bring us the missing cat, though sometimes it took as long as a day.

Speaking of Cozy Minaj, if reincarnation truly exists, she most certainly is a starlet come back to Hollywood. With her Marilyn Monroe beauty and seductiveness, complete with natural eyeliner and lipstick, she is the epitome of a femme fatale. This gorgeous white tabby has even developed a hoarse, wispy meow she uses when she really wants our attention.

She's also a real estate mogul. (Anthropomorphizing? Not by much, though I admit I have been known to ask her, "Where'd you get that nice coat, honey — Saks?") She would arrange boxes in the garage in such a way that she would have multiple rooms on the highest perch with the best view. She would even situate sheets of green flannel in front, emulating a green lawn in front of her hillside mansion. Eventually other cats became jealous and would take over her home, but that only encouraged her to build bigger and better.

The Cast of Characters

A few cats of the many we've cared for over twenty years are described in more detail here. These are the ones we've interacted with most closely. I might even say we've bonded with them, except that ferals don't normally bond with humans. Still, I'm almost certain I've seen them shoot a few winks my way once or twice. Or more likely, they just had something in their eye.

Grande Dame

I met the Grande Dame for the first time two decades ago, when the colony was already well established. She was a feral Siamese blend, clearly the alpha female. She and her mate, a large orange tabby we called Morris, were top of the family tree as far as our personal history with the colony was concerned.

We found her body gutted by a coyote on a neighbor's lawn five years later. Prior to her death, she gave birth to one particular cat that figures prominently in our colony's history, Marble.

Marble / Ghost of Marble

Marble is a robust, powerful tortoiseshell female with a wide face and deep, piercing, wise eyes. The care with which she has treated her litters won her a Mom of the Century Koscar Award — the first and only one ever given. The day she disappeared, it seemed more that she ascended than died, as she seemed destined for sainthood. So imagine our surprise when, one day years later, hidden in the bushes along the far reaches of the fence, there she stood again. And it wasn't one of her grown kittens; her markings had always been strikingly unique. This was so obviously an apparition that we decided to call her the Ghost of Marble. She has rejoined the colony, but we're still unsure if she's real or an apparition.

Since her return, the dynamic of the colony has changed. Alpha females that used to be subservient to her have asserted their power, and so she remains something of an outcast. Among her litters were four cats particularly important to the colony: Baby Gray, Shadow, Crazy Calico, and Snow White.

Baby Gray

Baby Gray is Tiny's mother, who abandoned her when Tiny was a kitten. Since Tiny regained her strength and grew into the formidable cat she is today, she has never forgiven her mother for forsaking her. Whenever she is outside, Tiny smacks her mother every chance she gets. Baby Gray is the only feral besides Tiny who brings us gifts. Rodents? No, clothing and children's toys! She also gave birth to Charlie and Princess, two cats with significant roles in the colony's history.

Like many mothers, Baby Gray has lost litters to predators. At times, she would carry her dead kittens by their nape, as if they were still alive. When we tried to remove the kittens, she would quickly move them elsewhere. She herself was nearly killed in an attack. The morning after, she came to show us her damaged paw, which the jaws of some assailant had latched onto, sticking it out for us to see. And every day after, she would show us how her paw was slowly healing.

She also gave birth to the Hello Kitties, three delightful feral kittens that, for some reason, connected with me the moment they heard my voice. They would pile against the fence, thinking they were hidden, when in fact they were fully exposed, small, furry rear ends sticking straight up in the air. But hearing my voice, they would unhuddle and run toward me. We brought them inside and contemplated keeping them. But they were still bonded with their mother, so we decided to leave them to their fate outside. One day, they wandered far into our neighbor's yard and couldn't find their way back. I tried coaxing them back with my voice, but they only made it halfway. The last we saw of them, they were playing in the neighbor's deep foliage; shortly after, they disappeared.

Shadow

The colony is matriarchal, so males rarely stick around for long. They tend to appear when the females go into heat and then leave on their own or are forced out by other males. The few males that have remained in the colony have been passive, with extremely mild temperaments. Shadow was a regal, pitch-black male and a close friend of Snow White's. Steady as an oak tree, he spent his entire life with the colony before dying of an infection.

Crazy Calico

Crazy Calico didn't live a particularly long life, but it was a strange one indeed. I've never seen a cat look and act as certifiably insane as she. Had she been human, our first impulse would have been to lock up all the sharp knives. Nothing came easy for her, especially giving birth. She had a nasty tendency of eating her young. From what we could tell, she didn't do it because the kittens in the litter were deformed or too weak, as sometimes happens, but just because she was nuts.

Nearly any kitten Crazy Calico didn't herself kill was soon predator fodder. Miraculously one puffball of a kitten did survive the carnage. But even he didn't come through unscathed. He ended up with a missing eye before he learned to climb to safety high in the trees. We called him One-Eyed Jack.

One-Eyed Jack

Born to a mother so inept that Child Services camped out on her front lawn, Jack teemed with frenetic energy. He hid up in the trees and made himself a nest there. Whenever he looked our way, he had to tilt his head, using his one good eye.

He was content playing alone in his tree house of branches and leaves, until one day he met Tiny. Being fierce, Tiny was not well liked in the colony and had not a single friend. But one day while exploring the jungle of our backyard, Tiny came upon One-Eyed Jack in the tree. Jack also had no friends, but for some reason, he was most welcoming when he met Tiny. They sniffed each other, and against all odds, became fast friends. They basked in the trees together, played chase among the branches, and even napped together. We relished this cat, though unfortunately his life wasn't a long one. He became a victim of predators.

Snow White

Snow White is a stunningly beautiful feral Siamese with a profound, quiet presence. Except for the time she brought her daughter Cozy back to us, she has never made a single noise. The shadowy patches on her neck that many Siamese share are said in feline folklore to originate from the thumbprints of gods who picked up the cats to admire them. She enjoys the companionship of the male tabby Charlie, promenading with him, rubbing against him during meals, and taking long afternoon naps in his arms. She has given birth to some of our finest cats, including Caliby, Jaguar, Boots, and the three sisters Bandy, Pierre, and Cozy.

Caliby

Like her name, Caliby is a mix of calico and tabby. On the small side and somewhat meek, she has outlived some of our more formidable cats. When riled, though, she puffs up her shoulders and can get quite nasty. And she has tremendous luck. First, she should've been easy prey for predators but somehow turned out to be one of the main colony's last survivors. Also, she once tucked herself into Sophie's engine bay and rode all the way to Sophie's work, thirty miles away. She stayed in the engine bay for nine hours and then rode all the way back home, without a scratch. Hearing faint mewing coming from the vicinity of the engine when she exited her car that night, Sophie immediately realized what had happened. She couldn't bring herself to open the hood, afraid of what she might find. So she had me do it instead. I discovered a very cozy-looking cat, completely unscathed, crying more from hunger than anything else.

Boots

Another of Snow White's kittens, Boots had a lush, steel-gray coat accented by white paws. She was the most fearful cat of the colony. This made sense, given that she was the daughter of Outsider. I was out of town when the male gray tabby Outsider showed up. When a new cat joined the family, it was always both an exciting and a nerve-racking moment. Would they upset the harmony of the colony? Would they fit in and be accepted?

My housemates named the newcomer Outsider, and I wondered why. They told me to just look outside. I peered through the blinds, and way off in the corner, as far from the colony as possible, sat a cat with guilt written all over his face. He knew he didn't belong there, and nothing we did to convince him otherwise would change that. He never fit in and didn't even try.

Boots shared his sense of alienation, though she didn't need to. We took great care to make her feel welcome. Still, the only way she would eat was to be fed separately from the others. To our surprise, one day she brought her new litter of kittens to us, carrying them one by one by the neck, to show them off. We were shocked, not only because she'd never looked pregnant, but because until then, we'd been fully convinced Boots was a male.

Her litter included a remarkable group of kittens, one more striking than the next. As expected, they were vulnerable, and we held midnight vigils to protect them, poised to scare away any predator that might try to pick them off. But when we dozed, the raccoons arrived, snatching a gorgeous feral Himalayan Siamese from the litter and decimating nearly all the rest. They left but one beautiful calico we called Gumdrop. Before she, too, could be lost, we brought her inside to safety. All night long, Boots and Gumdrop would call for each other through our back door. But as we learned time and again, knowing a kitten is safe is worth any amount of racket. During the day, we would let her out again to be with her mother, and then every night, we'd bring her in. Boots is no longer living; she was yet another victim of predators.

Gumdrop

The only pure calico of the colony, Gumdrop has the appearance of wearing a white onesie with patches of orange, brown, and black sewn on. I've often asked her whether that was the only outfit she came with. Her other name is Nurse Baby, for ever since she was a kitten, she has cared for any cat in distress. If one of our cats would get stuck on the roof or caught in a jam, she would run back and forth on the fence to get our attention — the feline equivalent of Lassie. If one of the cats had surgery, she would run to the cat when it came home and lick it. If that cat was in a cage, she would run around the cage, nuzzling whatever part of the injured cat she could reach through the steel mesh. Then she would lie alongside the cage, sleeping there all night to keep the other cat company. The most amazing thing: those she comforted were often her enemies. In a crisis, she had no bias.

817

One day, a large male calico we had never seen before lumbered into our yard like he owned it. He had the exact coloration of Gumdrop and was most certainly her father. It was not uncommon for males of litters to return once or twice to check on their broods. I surreptitiously followed him down our long driveway, then watched him cross the street, climb a tree leading to the second story of our neighbor's house, and enter through an open window. On the side of the house was the address in big black letters: 817. So from then on, he was known as 817. This is remarkable because most calicos are female. The rare male calico is sterile, due to Klinefelter's syndrome (having an additional X chromosome). A nonsterile male calico is basically unheard of.

Junior and Beige

No matter the amount of food around him, the infamous brat Junior, orange tabby runt of the litter, would call dibs on it all. He would use each of his four paws to cover as much food as he could, all the while gulping down as much of it as possible. If any other cat tried to horn in on his territory, which by his estimation was the entire backyard, he would growl and hiss and carry on. One day when he was a kitten, he somehow got himself stuck atop a thirty-five-foot telephone pole. How he eventually got down, we have no clue.

Beige was a littermate of Junior's. Beige disappeared soon after birth but, years later, returned as a full-grown male. He is one of only three males that have remained with the colony. He is a well-mannered and handsome cat. Though feral, he loves chasing a toy mouse on a string, as does Marble. When they see me bring the toy outside, they'll go into a deep downward-dog yoga stretch, then be ready to play.

Charlie and Princess

Charlie and Princess were the two surviving littermates of Baby Gray, though Princess didn't have a long life. (You'll learn more about Princess in chapter 16.) There was a third kitten in their litter, a lovely calico we named Patches. Baby Gray placed her brood behind the air-conditioning unit, where they were exposed to attack, no matter how we tried to dissuade her. When Patches was killed by predators one night, we brought the two remaining cats inside to keep them safe and named them Charlie and Princess.

Charlie became the bright-orange alpha male of the colony, loved by everyone, both male and female. When Charlie shows up, everyone gets excited. He's personable, friendly, and caring. As he grew and his orange color became more and more vivid, even his eyes turned orange. "Hope you like the color orange, Charlie" was the running joke. He is one solid muscle, extremely powerful and daring. But when he gets scared — sometimes by the smallest of things — Charlie begins to shake and runs to us for comfort.

His sister Princess we saved literally from the jaws of death. A raccoon had her by the neck, but we scared it into dropping her; remarkably she was left unscathed. She bonded strongly with Tiny, her stepsister. I wouldn't say the feeling was mutual. When we would put the two of them in the bathroom at night to sleep, Tiny always gave us a look of angst, while Princess looked at us with deep satisfaction. She would curl up against Tiny's body in total comfort. In the morning when we opened the bathroom door, Tiny couldn't wait to run from the room, but Princess was loath to let her go.

Other Males

Besides 817, we had our share of other males. Like traveling salesmen, they would bed our females, then hit the road. They included Sylvester, Midnight, Graystoke, Doppelganger (Charlie's evil twin), Spy, Clown, Scrappy Do (constant mange), Codad, and Thug, among others. No surprise, Thug was Tiny's father. He would run into our backyard without any warning and dive under the fence with arms extended, trying to kill anything he could snag. Not cats, but rodents or anything else that might be living there.

Once we named the cats, I felt as though our relationship with the colony had deepened. They never responded to their names or recognized inflection or sibilants, so I'm certain that sentiment was one-sided. From my viewpoint, though, naming them did seem to transform the relationship — from merely coexisting to being fully engaged with one another.

Boots with Gumdrop, her one surviving kitten.

10 From the Fertile Crescent to Hello Kitty

There was a historical precedent to the connection we felt with the cats. Ten thousand years ago or so in the Fertile Crescent, cats went from being merely functional to being embraced as pets. And by around 2000 BCE, they not only protected food stocks, but they protected human life from the poisonous snakes and scorpions that frequently entered homes in that region. Cats were welcomed indoors as pets in ancient Egypt, which is rather remarkable, given that keeping cats as indoor pets in the West is something of a new phenomenon — one that developed only in the past fifty years or so, with the advent of air conditioning and the invention of cat litter. In this relatively short time it has really caught on: one in three U.S. homes now has a cat. That's approximately one hundred million domestic cats in the United States alone. By some estimates, there could also be an equal number of ferals running wild.

American feral cats don't enjoy celebrity status like those of Italy, however. They are so esteemed there that a "biocultural heritage" law decrees that "wherever five or more cats live together in a 'natural urban habitat,' they can't be moved or chased away." It is estimated that in Rome alone there are three hundred thousand feral cats living in more than two thousand colonies.

Rome's city council is a strong advocate for these cats, too. It has acknowledged their ancient heritage, stating, "There is a deep-rooted affection for these cats who have an ancient bond with the city." They went even further in 2001, naming cats living in the Colosseum, the Forum, and Torre Argentina a part of the city's "bioheritage."

In the very place where Caesar was murdered is the sanctuary called Torre Argentina, where hundreds of feral cats live among Rome's earliest temples. These descendants of cats left behind thousands of years ago by the fallen empire moved into this protected area below street level. Traditionally they were cared for by the *gattare*, cat caretakers, usually older women of the neighborhood, the most famous being Italian film star Anna Magnani, who used to bring pots of pasta to feed the cats.

Unlike their lives of ease in the West today, cats worked for their keep in ancient Egypt. With granaries overflowing since his subjects were taxed in grain, the pharaoh had no choice but to put his kingdom's cats to work protecting this surplus of food. Not wanting to cause an uprising by demanding his subjects hand over their cats, he declared all cats demigods.

Mere humans couldn't own a demigod. That right belonged only to the pharaoh. So by deifying them, he was able to appropriate all the cats in one fell swoop. His subjects were now obligated to care for these demigods by day, bring them to the royal granaries each evening, and then pick them up again in the morning. And in doing so, they not only contributed to the well-being of the kingdom, but also received a tax credit.

Now that cats had attained divine status, new rules were implemented. Should a cat be killed or injured by a human, the culprit would be put to death. If a cat died of natural causes, a priest was required to examine its body to ensure that the death was indeed natural. Displays of grief when a cat died in a household would include effusive mourning, pounding on the chest, and shaving the eyebrows. The period of mourning was considered complete when the mourner's eyebrows had grown back. Should a house catch fire, cats were saved first, then if possible the other occupants.

Though it was illegal (under penalty of death) to remove a cat from Egypt — the equivalent of stealing from the pharaoh — cats still found their freedom. A government department was formed solely to deal with this issue, with agents dispatched to other lands to find and return cats that had been smuggled out of Egypt. But being proud and solitary creatures, cats could not even be controlled by the pharaoh.

The Egyptians made the mistake of extrapolating that if cats could protect granaries on land, why not on water? They could protect the food stores of vessels sailing up and down the Nile. A wonderful idea in theory — that is, until the boats docked. Then there was no keeping the cats from jumping ship and finding a home on another vessel. By 500 BCE, cats had migrated to every country bordering the Mediterranean Sea.

In no time, cats had gone from being functional to becoming pets to being revered as gods. If you could've bought stock in cats, you'd be retired. You'd just have to make sure you dumped your shares before cats were slaughtered by the millions, beginning in twelfth-century Europe, for being in league with the devil. By the way, instead of benefiting from their absence, Europe suffered. In the mid-fourteenth century, the black plague wiped out a third of its population. The plague spread more easily without cats there to kill the rats whose fleas spread the disease.

The problem for cats during the Middle Ages began when Pope Gregory IX ushered in the period of the Papal Inquisition in the mid-thirteenth century and, in his papal bull (edict) *Vox in Rama*, equated black cats with the devil. A frenzy of destroying black cats ensued, both to ensure that the devil wouldn't infiltrate the household and its residents, and to protect cat owners from accusations of being witches. Thus began a mass destruction of cats in Europe that essentially lasted five hundred years.

Pope Innocent VIII fueled this killing frenzy when he decreed in 1484 that all cats were unholy creatures and needed to be burned along with their owners, who were obviously witches. The devastation of cats during this period was without parallel. Especially black cats, which is the reason so few black cats are seen in Europe today.

In the seventeenth century, mechanical philosophy gained in popularity. This current of thought revived and further developed older philosophies of reductionism that proposed the universe could be explained in terms of mechanistic principles. This may explain, in part, why the widespread massacre of cats was tolerated. According to Cartesian philosophy, originated by René Descartes, animals were essentially machines.

Descartes planned to publish his thoughts on the operation of the material world in great detail. But he was aware of the condemnation suffered by Galileo, and concern over similar ecclesiastical reaction kept Descartes from publishing his tour de force, *Le Monde*. Still, parts of *Le Monde* (published posthumously) including the doctrine of the *bête-machine* (animal machine), did come to be known.

In his writings, Descartes posits that animals are not conscious. They do not have souls and, as such, are essentially automatons. They do not think, or reason, or have language. They have no self-consciousness and are without feeling. They act as if conscious, but in fact their reactions are merely mechanical. These reactions, while "much more splendid than artificial ones," are but the function of machines nonetheless.

He based his conclusions on experiments he and his adherents conducted, in which animals would be tortured in extreme ways. They concluded that the animals' excruciating reaction to torture was merely like that of a machine that needs fixing or a cog that needs oil. Since animals weren't sentient and felt no pain, there was no downside to destroying cats.

The murderers of cats, then, felt they were getting a moral pass. But after a hundred years of massacres, they had also succeeded at destroying the only barrier that existed between themselves and the black plague. Only when people began to notice that homes of those illegally hiding cats were being spared from the plague did opinions about cats begin to change. Word of this phenomenon spread, prompting a reconsideration of the original premise and eventually resulting in rats being designated as the culprits, not cats.

Laws enacted in order to destroy cats were repealed and replaced by edicts that now protected them. And, of course, everyone wanted a cat again. Thankfully cats are prolific breeders, and though they were nearly driven to extinction, their populations once again began to flourish.

Prior to Descartes's writings, however, skeptics had already begun voicing their opposition to violence against cats and questioning the scriptural basis for it. In the sixteenth century, Michel de Montaigne challenged the supposition that humans were more advanced than animals. In one of his essays he wrote, "When I play with my cat who knows whether I do not make her more sport than she makes me? We mutually divert one another with our play."

Hundreds of years before the Common Era, felines who took to the waves had an easier time of it. Invited aboard Phoenician and then Roman ships for their skill as mousers, cats witnessed the fall of Egypt and much of Europe, including Britain, at the hands of the Romans.

After arriving in Britain, one particular breed of cat made its way to Scandinavia. The breed was brought to Norway by the Vikings around 1000 CE during their voyages along trade routes with the Byzantine East. The Vikings, too, invited cats aboard to control vermin on their ships. Massive felines with an insulated, waterproof double coat, these cats were so admired by the Vikings they became legend. Freyja, the goddess of love, was said to ride a sled drawn by cats so formidable even Thor himself couldn't pick them up. Even today, this breed, known as the Norwegian Forest cat, is highly muscled, powerful, and robust, certainly a fine complement to the Vikings and worthy of the myth that surrounds them. The Danes also held them in awe, calling them *Huldrekat*, or "female forest spirits."

Felines on sailing vessels became a common theme. They accompanied Christopher Columbus to the Americas, and even Louis XIV required by law that every vessel carry two ship cats. During the European colonization of the Americas, polydactyl cats (those having more than the usual number of toes) proved to be exceptional mousers and so were preferred. This accounts for the high incidence of polydactyly on the East Coast, where the original colonies were established.

It was so advantageous to have cats aboard that the ship cat became something of an institution. Even the U.S. Naval Institute has acknowledged cats' contribution on ships, with pictures and names of cats honored for their service displayed on its website.

The symbiotic relationship between ship cat and crew had at its foundation the same pact made when cats were first lured from the wild: the prospect of easy prey in exchange for guarding surplus food stocks. On sailing vessels, cats not only protected food supplies from rodents, but also protected the crew from the diseases that rodents carried. Keeping rodents under control also meant that rope, sails, and rigging would be safe from gnawing vermin. But there was more to the relationship than that. It began as analytical, even superstitious: studying cats' moods to predict the weather, or noticing whether the cat licked its fur against the grain, indicating an imminent hailstorm.

Then the relationship deepened. Ship cats were embraced as companions. As ship mascots. They were recognized for their beauty, innocence, intelligence, and warmth. A reminder of home in the midst of war, perilous weather, or long stretches at sea — with the added benefit that ship cats pulled their own weight.

In March 1943, Eugene Clancy and five of his crewmen were torpedoed in the North Atlantic and left floating on a life raft for fifty-six days along with ship cat Maizie. Clancy said, "If Maizie hadn't been with us, we might have gone nuts. We completely forgot our personal discomfort and almost fought for the privilege of petting her. Maizie... even comforted those suffering from exposure or seasickness by going from one to another almost like a mother."

There are many such stories of heroic ship cats. The crew of the British frigate *Amethyst*, for instance, finding itself under siege by Chinese artillery in 1949 and having run aground up the Yangtze River, credited their survival to Simon, their black-and-white ship cat. Simon protected their food stocks against marauding rats for three months until the ship could be repaired. Simon was also credited with keeping the crew's spirits up through the ordeal. Even being severely injured himself during the battle didn't keep Simon from his duties. He was given the Dickin Medal for his heroics, the equivalent of the Victoria Cross for animals. He was the first and only cat to receive such an honor. Tragically he succumbed to his injuries on returning to the UK.

Another cat, named U-boat, was aboard a Royal Navy vessel during World War II and would take shore leave whenever his ship came into port. He would spend days onshore, usually returning only just before his ship sailed. One day, U-boat failed to return in time for roll call, and his ship was forced to sail. As the ship pulled away from the quay, U-boat was seen running down the dock after the departing ship. He made a death-defying leap onto the ship and succeeded in making it aboard. He was reported to be undaunted by his experience, proceeding to wash himself on deck. The crew members were reportedly delighted their good-luck charm had returned.

The idea of cat as talisman reflects ancient traditions regarding ship cats. Some mariners believed storms could be conjured through magic stored in a cat's tail. According to another superstition, if a cat approached a sailor on deck, it was an auspicious omen; but if the cat came only halfway and retreated, the opposite was true. The crew of the RMS *Empress of Ireland* should have heeded that particular superstition. Emmy was their ship cat, an orange tabby who, until May 28, 1914, never missed a voyage. On that day, however, Emmy began acting strangely, trying to escape the ship before departure, until she finally succeeded in running onto dry land. The distraught crew did everything they could to coax her back aboard, but eventually the *Empress* had to leave without her. She was reportedly last seen on the roof of a shed on the pier, watching her ship sail out of Quebec City. Early the next morning, the *Empress* collided with the SS *Storstad* while steaming through fog at the mouth of the Saint Lawrence River and rapidly sank, killing over a thousand people.

An homage to ship cats was depicted in the 1979 film *Alien.* Warrant officer Ellen Ripley's pet cat, a ginger tabby named Jones, was kept aboard the spaceship to control rodents. According to the author of the novelized version of the movie, the cat also served as a source of relaxation and entertainment for the crew on long space journeys. Ripley and Jones being sequestered together in hypersleep for fifty-seven years is also reminiscent of tombs from the ancient past where pet owner and pet have been discovered buried together side by side.

Cats ingratiated themselves almost everywhere sailing vessels took them, including the Islamic world. They were particularly revered in the Middle East among scholars, who wrote odes to cats, not just in appreciation for protecting their stored food, but for keeping their precious books safe from vermin. Their purrs were compared to the *dhikr,* the rhythmic chanting of the Sufis, used in healing in early Islamic hospitals.

And for good reason. Most cat purrs fall within the anabolic frequencies of 20 to 50 Hz, and some go up to 140 Hz (anabolic hormones stimulate protein synthesis, muscle growth, and insulin); according to recent scientific studies, these frequencies promote healing. Three species of cats purr at precisely 120 Hz, a frequency that has been found to repair tendons. A purring cat can lower blood pressure, relieve stress, and help heal infection, swelling, and even soft tissue injuries. Cat owners may have up to 40 percent less risk of heart attack and stroke. And there may be truth to the old veterinary adage "If you put a cat and a bunch of broken bones in the same room, the bones will heal," since bone repair is stimulated at the very frequencies at which cats purr. For those familiar with David Hawkins's calibration list, he gauges a cat's purr to be 500, the vibration of unconditional love.

In Islamic culture, cats were also known catalysts for life

transformation, as described in one instance in the hadiths (reports of deeds and sayings of Muhammad):

> The grammarian Ibn Babshad was sitting with his friends on the roof of a mosque in Cairo, eating some food. When a cat passed by they gave her some morsels; she took them and ran away, only to come back time and time again. The scholars followed her and saw her running to an adjacent house on whose roof a blind cat was sitting. The cat carefully placed the morsels in front of the helpless feline. Babshad was so moved by God's caring for the blind creature that he gave up all his belongings and lived in poverty, completely trusting in God until he died in 1067.

Another story is told of Sufi master Shaykh Abu Bakr al-Shibli, who when he passed away in 945 CE appeared to his friend in a dream:

> On being asked [by his friend] what Allah had done to him, he said that he had been granted admission to Paradise, but was asked by Allah if he knew the reason for this blessing. Shaykh Shibli enumerated all his religious duties but none of his acts of piety had saved him. Finally Allah asked him, "Do you remember the cold day in Baghdad when it was snowing and you were walking in your coat when you saw a tiny kitten on a wall shivering with cold, and you took it and put it under your warm coat? For the sake of this kitten We have forgiven you."

Muhammad was said to have had a great fondness for cats, especially his favorite, Muezza, whom he let rest on his lap while he gave sermons. He even performed ablutions from water drunk by a cat, which normally would've been considered an unclean act. Muhammad allowed a cat to give birth on his cloak, and even cut off the sleeves of his favorite prayer robe rather than wake Muezza, who was sleeping on it.

Whether or not Muhammad actually said that "a love of cats is an aspect of faith" or, as described in the hadiths, that a woman who locked up her cat and refused to feed it after being scratched would be tortured in hell for all eternity, these reports do reflect the esteem in which cats were held in the Islamic world. Ironically this was at a time when they were being destroyed in Europe. Even today, cats are generally admired by Muslims, if for no other reason than Muhammad's affinity for them and their inclusion in many hadiths.

Muhammad even gave his close companion Abd al-Shams the nickname Abu Hurayrah (Father of the Kitten). Although the word *cat* originates from the Arabic word *qit*, because Abu had deep affection for his male kitten, which he always carried in his bag, he was given the name for "male kitten" (*hurayrah*) instead.

According to legend, Abu's kitten saved Muhammad from a deadly snake. The grateful prophet stroked the cat's back and forehead, thus blessing all cats with the righting reflex (the ability to orient itself as it falls, in order to land on its feet), and the stripes some cats have on their foreheads are believed to mark the touch of Muhammad's fingers.

The story is told somewhat differently in Christian folklore. The Virgin Mary blessed a cat that had killed a venomous snake sent by the devil to bite the Christ child in his crib. Another story tells of the infant Jesus lying in the manger shivering from cold. Alerted by his cries, a mother tabby cat lay next to the child to warm him. In gratitude, Mary stroked the cat's forehead, marking it with an *M*, and to this day, the caring mother cat's descendants all carry the mark of Mary.

Cats were also revered in both China and Japan. Not only were agricultural deities depicted as cats there, but delicate and finely executed watercolors on parchment and silk indicated cats' importance. They also resided as pets in the royal palaces.

The Chinese goddess Li Shou, associated with fertility and vermin control, was portrayed in cat form. Even the gods turned to her when they needed help running the world.

According to ancient Chinese mythology, the gods who created the earth decided they needed someone to oversee their new creation to ensure that things would run smoothly. After considering each creature, they offered the job to the goddess Li Shou — a cat. She and her fellow cats gladly accepted, and in return were given the power of speech. So roam the world they did, and order was maintained. That is, until Li Shou came upon a cherry tree. After curling up for a short nap, she was abruptly awakened by the gods towering over her, blaming her for the world falling into chaos while she slept. She promised apologetically that it would never happen again. And yet the inviting tree lured her back under its welcome shade and dropped soft cherry blossoms on her face as she dozed off. Once again she was reprimanded by the gods. This time she made a solemn vow not to sleep on the job, but then falling cherry blossoms diverted her attention and she danced after them.

Realizing that cats were incapable of maintaining order in the world, the gods took from them the power of speech and gave it to humans, and placed humans in charge. But since cats had been their first choice, the gods imbued them with the power of controlling the sun's movement, and thus timekeeping. Even today it's said that one can tell the time by looking into a cat's eyes.

In Japan, cats gained favor by protecting worms used for making silk. There is a small cat shrine built in the middle of the island of Tashirojima, where silkworms were raised beginning in the mid-eighteenth century. The shrine honors cats' ability to protect silkworm farms from mice. Today, the local population of one hundred humans is dwarfed by the number of cats on the island. Residents feel that the cats not only help predict weather patterns, but bring them luck and prosperity.

And arising from the mysterious qualities cats possess came the legend of the *bakeneko*, a supernatural creature a cat would transform into when it lived to a certain age. It was said to grow another tail, stand erect, and speak in a human language. Apparently the legend grew out of people's fascination with the way a cat's iris changes shape depending on the time of day; the way their fur sparks with static electricity when petted; the way they licked fish oil; the way they walk without making a sound; the fact that they were difficult to control; and the sharpness of their claws and teeth.

Of course, there is also the popular cult of *maneki-neko*, which began in the late-nineteenth-century in Japan. There are differing folktales as to the origin of the waving cat (though it is in fact beckoning), mostly around the theme of the cat saving the life of a prominent person — sometimes a priest, other times a Samurai leader — who becomes captivated by the beckoning cat. Just as they move toward the inviting cat, a bolt of lightning strikes exactly where they had been standing. It remains a very popular talisman of good fortune. Some people believe the ubiquitous Hello Kitty has its origins in *maneki-neko*, though its creator, Yuko Shimizu, has said instead that she was inspired by Lewis Carroll's *Through the Looking-Glass*, where in a scene early in the book, Alice plays with a cat she calls Kitty. The whole idea was about social communication, but ironically Hello Kitty does not have a mouth. The explanation is that the cat speaks from the heart.

Two feral kittens exploring the back yard.

11 Protecting the Colony

"We now have three brand new litters, one by the faucet, one by the garbage cans, one in the yard behind ours...nonstop action, plants knocked over, ants everywhere, Tiny just barfed her dry food, now everybody is clawing on the banister, crying new babies outside, stay away as long as humanly possible, it's craaaaaaaaaaaaaazy here!"
— My text to Sophie when she was out of town,
August 12, 2009

There are inherent challenges in maintaining a secret family of cats. One can't brag about newborns to the neighbors or expect them to commiserate with you about your family tragedies. One must remain completely disinterested when the cats are visible, since a neighbor might be watching. The cats must be fed and cared for in private. Runs to the vet are done under cover of darkness or with the cats in draped cages in the backseat, hidden from prying eyes. Oversized bags of dried cat food, forty-pound boxes of kitty litter, and stashes of canned food must be hurried into the house, hidden under twelve-pack rolls of paper towels.

And then the cats must learn. When the screen door of the neighbor's house slams shut and the shuffle of slippers comes their way, they must scatter. Or when the creak of a back door is followed by the sound of a chain quickly unfurling, the pit bull next door will race to snag any cat that didn't recognize that sound (and the neighbor never understands why their dog always charges our fence). Everything is done under a cloak of secrecy. Even when old or sick cats from the colony leave to die, it is done without anyone being the wiser. No body would ever be found, no scent of a rotting carcass ever smelled. I'm the Charles Lindbergh of my neighborhood, maintaining a secret family nobody will ever know about.

Since we'd begun feeding the colony, we were seeing stronger and healthier litters, perhaps four litters every three months. Twice a day, along the slab of concrete located outside our back door, I put out premium kibbles for the waiting colony, occasionally adding canned food, especially on weekends and holidays. I spread out the food smorgasbord style, making special accommodations for those cats that liked to eat alone, and made sure their water bowls were always cleaned and filled. Once they were done eating, I would clean any remaining scraps of food from the concrete and late at night would hose down the eating area.

I was spending two hundred dollars a month on cat food. (Though my housemates and I shared the responsibility of caring for the cats, I got stuck with litter-box cleaning and the food and vet bills.) I enjoyed teasing the cats while they ate: "Here I am working my fingers to the bone just to keep you kids fed and clothed, and I don't even get a thanks. Not even eye contact."

Being properly nourished now, mothers had more strength and so weren't abandoning their kittens as before. But that didn't keep Crazy Calico from her madness. Sophie happened to walk by the screen door one day when I wasn't home, just as Crazy spun around, screamed, and birthed a litter of kittens right in plain view. She quickly ate one (or was it the placenta?) before running off, dragging the rest by their umbilical cords.

"That," Sophie said in no uncertain terms, "I could've done without seeing."

When I returned late that night, Crazy was still dragging her kittens around by their umbilical cords. So at 1:00 AM I sterilized a sharp knife over the stove and gently approached them. She must've known I was there to help, because ordinarily Crazy would never have let me get this close to her. I felt for where the cord had already dried out and cut away sections, eventually freeing the kittens from their mother, who quickly ran away. Then I noticed that the remaining cord had wrapped itself around the newborns, smothering them. I quickly cut away the cord and unwound it from their necks and bodies, careful not to touch the kittens directly.

What might have seemed overwhelming when I first became involved with the cats was now just a matter of course. Nothing seemed too much to handle. Anything short of death seemed workable.

The next morning, I saw Crazy reunited with her kittens, and all seemed right with the world. That is, until she grabbed each by the scruff of the neck, jumped up on the box that housed our utility meters, located in an alcove on the side of our house, and dropped them through a small hole there to keep them safe. Shaking my head, I quietly went outside and had a heart-to-heart with dear Crazy.

"How do you expect to get them out of there?" I asked her.

She held my gaze.

"Unless you have elasto-paws, there's no way you'll be able to reach your babies."

She looked over at the utility box, seemingly considering this.

"And there's no way in hell they'll be able to crawl out of that pit you just dropped them in."

Already the kittens were calling for their mother. Jumping onto the utility box, peering into the deep hole, Crazy realized her predicament. Frankly I was relieved. Having her kittens out of reach meant none would be missing ears, legs, eyes, or anything else, for the time being.

But they did need nourishment. So I took a crowbar and broke open the entire structure while Crazy watched. I was finally able to reach in and grab the kittens, which I did with paper towels so as not to get my scent on them. Between being smothered by their umbilical cords and dropped into a hole, they had already burned through two of their nine lives in less than twenty-four hours. I only partially repaired the utility box in case another mother had the same idea; now I would have easy access to otherwise impossible-to-reach kittens.

I watched Crazy carefully, and that gleam in her eye worried me. She didn't respond to her crying litter, so I nudged them toward another lactating female who had recently lost a litter and was watching nearby. She began nursing them as her own. Crazy seemed content just to saunter away, and we were finally left with a fighting chance for a litter of hers to survive intact.

That night, neighborhood dogs began barking in staggered succession, indicating predators on the prowl. I ran to the street and spotted a pack of coyotes. They would gingerly jog along, then speed up and rush down any driveway they chose. Then they would disappear, certainly in search of prey, before reemerging and trying another driveway. They looked my way and cowered, having learned their lesson about this address — the bastards (sorry).

But that didn't keep them from visiting my next-door neighbor, whose domestic cat happened to be outside. This cat had obviously never seen a coyote before and, being curious, carefully approached the prone, salivating wild animal. Well, I broke up that party in a hurry, much to the coyote's dismay.

Now that the colony was well fed and relatively safe from predators, my biggest challenge was keeping kittens safe when I wasn't there to protect them. Mothers gave birth out of sight. They prepared birthing sanctuaries ahead of time in the deep underbrush far from view, often on the rear neighbor's side of the fence. But once they determined their brood had matured enough to be shown off, they would present them to us. Proud mothers displaying their litters. Those days were remarkable. A small white head would pop out of the grass, then an orange one, then a black one. Fresh new life, a world of possibilities. And it gave me ulcers.

Had they remained in their sanctuaries, the kittens would've remained safe. But on our side of the fence, the deep underbrush thinned, making them more vulnerable. I noticed that mothers tended to move their kittens back to their birthing nests at night and then bring them out again during the day. So I bought long strips of six-inch-wide metal flashing and attached them to the bottom of the fence that surrounded our property. This covered the gaps between the ground and the fence, making it impossible for a kitten to pass through. And I plugged the occasional large hole between our yard and the jungle behind with large rocks. Mothers could come and go by climbing the fence, but their kittens could not.

I continued feeding the colony breakfast as usual, while newborn kittens called for their mothers from behind the sheet metal. Then I'd remove the stones from holes through which kittens would rush into our yard to be reunited with their mothers. At night when mothers put their broods away again, the holes were closed up, and the cycle repeated. This technique worked wonderfully. That is, until the kittens became stronger. When I stopped hearing the kittens calling for their mothers, I knew I was screwed. I spied small heads and paws peeking at me from over the seven-foot-tall fence and realized the kittens could now climb the fence at will.

Since I couldn't monitor the colony around the clock, and could no longer restrict access to the newborns, I considered other ways of keeping them safe from predators. I tried a rotating sprinkler, but that soaked the ground too much, making a mess.

A friend told me about wild horses he once raised in Northern California and how he'd had trouble with cougars attacking his foals. He set up hay bales around his property doused with lion urine he obtained from a local zoo, and that was the end of his cougar problem. The urine of bears and other types of predators is available for sale (from Pee Mart — I kid you not), along with raccoon deterrent sprays. I thought of using them but was afraid they would harm the cats, or at least cause them disorientation or distress.

But I was clear about one thing: the kids from the apartments next door who had recently begun teasing and throwing plastic bottles at my cats — yes, they were now *my* cats — and climbing over the fence and spying into my yard were about to be read the riot act. I asked them why they would do such a thing to such small, precious animals but got nothing back but attitude.

They merely reflected back to me what a jerk I had been at their age, and perhaps still am. I was the boy who killed a lizard with a slingshot just to see what would happen. I neglected my pet black rabbit, Thumper, when I got tired of feeding him. Angry with myself — and at the kids for making me remember how mean I, too, have been to animals — I crossed to the apartment complex next door, carrying the large sheet-metal shears I still had in my hand from repairing the flashing. Swinging the shears, I yelled that whoever's kids these were better keep them away from my cats. People peered through blinds. Certain I was about to go postal, somebody called the kids inside, and I never had a problem with them again. Clearly, Crazy Calico had been a bad influence on me.

Such outrageous behavior did, thankfully, cause me to reflect. My desire to do anything I could for these cats was perhaps fueled by my having failed at so many things I'd attempted in my life. I just wanted to do this one thing right. This was coupled with my growing respect and admiration for these animals and the bond I felt between us. Much of life and human interaction baffles me, but this relationship made sense. This relationship I understood.

I could see why cats were worshipped in ancient Egypt. There powerful feline goddesses appeared, beginning with Mafdet in the early dynastic period around 3000 BCE. The goddess Bastet was even represented by the domestic cat. The visiting Greek historian Herodotus noted that an enormous temple complex was built in Bastet's honor in the center of the city, and having participated in a festival honoring her, he reported it to be the largest and most enthusiastic celebration in all of Egypt.

The Egyptians' reverence for cats was so great that, in a decisive battle in the sixth century BCE, they let a city fall to the

Persians rather than risk harming cats. As the *Ancient History Encyclopedia* describes it:

> The greatest example of Egyptian devotion to the cat, however, comes from the Battle of Pelusium (525 BCE) in which Cambyses II of Persia defeated the forces of the Egyptian Pharaoh Psametik III to conquer Egypt. Knowing of the Egyptian's love for cats, Cambyses had his men round up various animals, cats chiefly among them, and drive the animals before the invading forces toward the fortified city of Pelusium on the Nile. The Persian soldiers painted images of cats on their shields, and may have held cats in their arms, as they marched behind the wall of animals. The Egyptians, reluctant to defend themselves for fear of harming the cats (and perhaps incurring the death penalty should they kill one), and demoralized at seeing the image of Bastet on the enemy's shields, surrendered the city and let Egypt fall to the Persians. The historian Polyaenus (2nd century CE) writes that, after the surrender, Cambyses rode in triumph through the city and hurled cats into the faces of the defeated Egyptians in scorn.

Taking stock, I felt I had tipped the scales somewhat in the colony's favor. But that's only because I forgot how adaptable nature can be. Just when I thought I had a handle on predators, an entirely new breed of raccoon showed up. Like mutants raised in a toxic waste dump.

Sitting outside with the colony one evening, I became aware that things had suddenly become deathly quiet. Not a leaf rustle could be heard. Then I noticed the cats all turn their heads slowly, having spotted something behind me. Their eyes widened, and my blood turned cold while I wondered what I might see if I turned around. It had to be something scary, because a normal spooky moment would've caused the colony to scatter. But here they sat, too scared to flee.

Stark terror has no self-reflection. There is no analyzing, no weighing options, no inner dialogue. That only happens in retrospect. I once rented a room in Nepal. It was located near an old, decrepit home I had been warned was haunted by a malevolent female spirit. Admittedly I'd taken that news in stride. But it did make me wonder why the room was so cheap and no one else wanted it. So rent it I did.

Well, not two weeks later, I heard a knock on my door late at night. The door consisted of two tall pieces of teak cut down the middle and secured from the inside with a thick horizontal iron bar. I peered through the drapes next to the door, and under the porch light didn't see a soul. More knocks on the door, louder and more insistent. Again, nobody seen. Then a bone-chilling woman's shriek and a thunderous crash against my door, as if a very large person had thrown their body against it. I watched in amazement as the force continued, slowly bending the thick metal bar that secured the doors, hinges creaking from the sides, ready to implode. I glanced once more out the window, the doors nearly splitting now, and nobody was there. Scared? I nearly fainted.

A man from upstairs heard the commotion and called out to see what was causing all the racket. Whatever had been pressing against my door suddenly stopped, and I heard noises of something racing up the stairs, then bursting into the room upstairs. I heard the man's screams, things flying across the room and smashing against his walls, and what sounded like the bed being upended and tossed around the room like a toy. Had I not been completely frozen in fear, I might have tried to help.

Now, seeing the cats' reaction to whatever was behind me, I knew I had no choice but to look. So turn I did, with squinted eyes.

There crouched three raccoons. The two in front were the size of grizzly bears, teeth bared, silent as death. Until they growled at me, a deep, guttural "wait till your father comes home" snarl straight out of the Miocene epoch. And those were just the two in front. Behind them sat an anomaly: like Nessie or the Yeti — something likely never to be seen again — a raccoon easily the size of a Buick Electra. The big model, like 1973.

I held up one hand, keeping the monster raccoons engaged by wiggling my fingers, then snapped the fingers of my other hand at the colony, bringing them to their senses and causing the cats to scatter like smoke. I was cornered. Usually I had a safety plan, but these beasts had shown up without warning. I slowly rose from my seat and crept on top of the large air-conditioning unit to see their reaction. This way I could increase my size while putting myself within climbing distance of the utility box — if necessary, I would be safe there (until my bones were found years later). I slowly climbed higher and didn't notice any aggression, so I gently widened my arm span, making myself as large as possible, keeping my energy quiet so as not to be deemed a threat. Eventually they seemed to get bored more than anything else and slowly lumbered back the way they came. Except for the Buick, who virtually stepped over the seven-foot fence in a single step. Damn, large *and* fast.

Now that I knew a portal from hell had opened and deposited demon raccoons in the neighborhood, I had to up my game. And the timing couldn't have been worse.

Snow White, our stunning Siamese feral, has a luxuriant white coat accented by sparkling blue eyes the color of sapphires. She is one of the few mothers who keeps constant contact with cats from her previous litters. Though many have been killed, she seems to relish her time with those who have survived, as if appreciating the preciousness of life. That's my imagination speaking.

She and her fully grown daughters Caliby and Boots often stayed together, grooming and caring for one another. Soon after the monster raccoons made their appearance, Snow White had another litter, survived by a single kitten. This cat had a silver-furred, leopard-spotted coat the likes of which we had never before seen. We called him Jaguar.

Snow White adored this creature more than any mother in the colony had ever loved any kitten. She would smother him with love, calling out to him whenever he had strayed even inches away. They called for each other constantly. She would pull him into her arms and lick him every chance she got. His coat of fur was so radiant I was mesmerized, imagining what it would be like just to touch it. Typical of males in the colony, he would venture out and explore but always come running at the first sound of his mother's call.

One evening, I went out to feed the cats, and none were to be seen — a bad sign. Out of the corner of my eye, I glimpsed the grizzly raccoons! And one had just grabbed Snow White's prized kitten, running with him in its jaws; the kitten's screams were horrific. I raced after them screaming, "No! No!" at the top of my lungs. Neighbors rushed out, alarmed. I was not going to lose that cat. I tripped over plumbing supplies stored in the neighbor's yard, then raced down a narrow alcove, almost on the raccoon now. Seeing me closing in, the raccoon dropped Jaguar, but not before severely injuring him. I stood there, breathless, devastated, looking down at him. He tried to meow, but only a death knell passed between his lips. The neighbors gathered around, whispering, "Gatito" ("kitten" in Spanish). I carried the decimated creature back to the house.

Holding him as I walked, I realized that I had finally gotten a chance to feel his fur, but of course not the way I had wanted.

I laid his body down as he took his last breaths, and said prayers for this lovely being as he passed away.

As was always the case whenever a tragedy like this struck, the entire backyard was solemn the next morning, the air thick with mourning. When I found Snow White hiding in the bushes, our gazes met, and I saw that her stunning blue eyes had changed to gray. To this day, her eyes have never displayed their brilliant blue again.

Cats soon took over the human beds.

12 Interrupting the Cycle

D espite the tragedy of losing kittens, the colony was growing. The cycles of birth, life, and death had taken place within this colony long before we arrived and would continue long after we were gone. To interfere in significant ways with that rhythm seemed almost a crime against nature. But after Snow White lost Jaguar, I said enough is enough. It had been three intense years of nurturing, protecting, and caring, and years prior to that of helping where I could. I wasn't going to watch another kitten die like that. Plus I was exhausted, both physically and emotionally. Mothers of the colony looked weary, too. The toll of having multiple litters was apparent.

I wondered about disbanding the colony. I called local animal shelters and humane societies to discuss this option and was surprised to hear they wouldn't accept feral cats. They explained that any feral cats they do receive are euthanized, as they are asocial and simply not adoptable; it was hard enough for them to place domestic cats left in their care. That's when the idea of neutering the colony first came to mind.

Now it seems so logical, but at the time, we were torn about interfering with nature to that degree. It was one thing to provide our colony nourishing food and whatever protection we could, and quite another to take from them their ability to give birth. When I thought back on the cycle of life we witnessed — males arriving to court the females, pregnant mothers giving birth and purposefully caring for their brood, and the interplay between kittens and their mothers — I concluded that the decision to end that possibility for them shouldn't be mine to make.

Then I heard about Disneyland's feral-cat colony. More than two hundred feral cats have called Disneyland home for decades, with sightings of ferals there going back as far as 1955. By the management's own admission, the park is glad to have them, calling them natural exterminators. Being feral, cats there have no contact with the public, but they are properly nourished at feeding stations situated throughout the park. In 2008, Disneyland contacted a community-based organization called FixNation to trap, neuter, and release the resident cats (an approach known as "TNR"), which they described as "a lasting protocol for the humane care of the resort's cats."

At the time, I didn't know what TNR meant, but "humane care" sounded good. And if it was okay at Uncle Walt's place, it was okay at mine. I felt better knowing it had taken Disneyland more than fifty years to implement TNR, just as it had taken me years of struggling with my colony's well-being before considering it.

Once I looked into it, I discovered an entire microcosm of organizations worldwide, along with their thousands of volunteers, that help support feral-cat colonies. They educate caretakers and the general public about feral cats; offer neutering and medical services; lobby for feral-cat rights; cooperate with those concerned about the safety of birds and other indigenous creatures; and work on solutions when feral-cat colonies become a nuisance. There are also no-kill cat sanctuaries that will accept feral cats, caring for them for life, in many cases outside the confines of cages, allowing the cats to run free in large homes or on properties with large yards.

An example of the passion behind such caregiving is obvious from a paragraph posted, in one variation or another, on many feral-cat-rescue websites:

> Feral Cats: They live in the shadows — the alleyways, empty lots and condemned buildings of almost every neighborhood. Their lives are short and usually harsh. They struggle to find food and water in an environment filled with the constant threats of disease, starvation, cruelty, and predation. They are the abandoned, the lost and the wild — and they need our help.... Our work is never done, our homes are never quiet, our wallets are always empty but our hearts are always full.

The key to maintaining a manageable feral colony, it seems, is having every member of the colony neutered when they come of age. The Stanford University Cat Network reduced its feral population from as many as 1,500 cats to 300 over a ten-year period by implementing TNR. Using TNR and adoptions, the Southern Animal Foundation reduced a feral-cat population in New Orleans from 500 to 65 in three years.

I learned that FixNation was but one of many feral-cat aid

organizations, and they're all in agreement that my initial idea of disbanding the colony would've been a mistake. Their extensive studies indicate that removing colonies altogether creates a vacuum that will only be filled with new feral colonies, since feral cats are attracted by food and shelter, whether it's offered by a caregiver or nature itself. Also, rodents tend to thrive when their predators are removed.

The idea is that newly fixed feral cats are to be returned to the exact spot where they were trapped, where they are then allowed to live out the rest of their lives. This approach works because fixing the cats ends the cycle of kittens being born, so the population stabilizes and, over time, decreases naturally.

I contacted FixNation and was told they would neuter our feral cats at no cost. Remarkable, since it would've been impossible to afford neutering all our cats otherwise. Because of the large number of cats they fix, FixNation required that appointments be made well in advance (though they have since changed their policies and now offer day-of-surgery appointments). I was also made aware there was a step-by-step, veterinarian-sanctioned protocol that needed to be followed prior to the surgery; otherwise, the procedure would need to be postponed.

First, the cat must be trapped in a secure cage that is designed with the cat's safety in mind, free of any sharp edges that might harm a frightened kitty. They recommended traps made by a company called Tomahawk; if I didn't have one of my own, they were happy to loan me one. These humane traps were also for *my* safety and that of the clinic's vets and staff as well. If more than one cat ended up caught in the trap, I would need a separate trap for each cat to transport them home postsurgery. The clinic also kindly loaned me a fitted cover that went over the entire trap; blocking out the view with it would help soothe the captured critter and help reduce stress and anxiety.

Once trapped, any cat older than four months wouldn't be

allowed to eat anything after midnight the night prior to the surgery, as anesthesia can only be safely performed when the stomach is completely empty.

Finally I also had to agree for each cat to be ear tipped. A snipped ear, which they assured me was not painful for the cat, was the universal sign that a feral cat had been neutered. This not only prevented confusion as to a cat's breeding status, but signaled that the colony was being cared for by someone, that these were not destitute cats fending for themselves.

I remember poring over the FixNation literature in my room and reading that requirement for ear tipping. I cringed. Gumdrop happened to be in my room, with Charlie sitting next to her. I looked closely at their ears, and they were perfect, not a single nick. It pained me to imagine agreeing to mutilation, albeit minor. I imagined Charlie saying, "What, you took my balls, and you still want a piece of ear?"

I continued reading. "You must be on time bringing the cats in for surgery, or you will be turned away. Any evidence of food in the cage, and your cat will be turned away." I was already nervous and now was getting more so. Would I remember everything? How was I going to catch every cat? I felt certain that with the huge number of feral cats they handled in the stressful situation of being neutered, following protocol was imperative. (FixNation provides free training for all first-time trappers, but unfortunately I wasn't aware of it at the time.)

I remembered walks I used to take through Ocean Park in Santa Monica. High bluffs stand picturesquely above the Pacific, and many people enjoy strolling or jogging along the paths there. Every evening near sunset, a group of people would pull up in their cars, bringing with them containers of food, shovels to remove cat waste, and water bottles — a real orchestration. As soon as they arrived, feral cats hidden in the bluffs would come running. They seemed familiar with the routine. When the volunteers were finished caring for this colony, they moved on to the next feral colony down the road. I marveled at their commitment and frankly also thought they seemed a little nuts. Now I realized I had become a whack job, too. I was in knee deep.

I was now certain neutering the colony was absolutely the right decision for everyone involved. I had my first appointment scheduled in two days, and everything was set. If I couldn't snare a cat, I could still cancel. Still, I wanted a sign. A sign from the universe that this was the right choice. I waited and waited, and no sign was forthcoming. I stayed up half the night, and still nothing.

The next morning, I opened the back door to feed the cats breakfast, as I always did, and in walked Baby Gray. Right into the house. In all the years prior and since, no feral cat from the colony has ever entered the house, except for the ones we saved from predators and hand-raised. She jumped up on the kitchen windowsill and waited. I ran into the garage and grabbed the cage, pinching myself to see if I was dreaming. I rested the cage on the counter. Then, as I moved toward her, she nonchalantly entered, and I locked the door behind her. She turned out to be the easiest cat I ever caught. My first customer. What could be a better sign than that? We're on.

I kept her caged in the garage that day, making sure she was well fed and as comfortable as possible. The rest of the colony was skittish. They all knew something was up. I made sure not to feed Baby Gray late at night and removed all remnants of food from the cage. I refilled her water dish and bid her good night.

The next morning, I drove to the facility, as nervous as a mother dropping off her child for its first day of nursery school. Shaking inside as I pulled up, I saw trucks, vans, and cars loaded to the gills with cages full of feral cats. I even saw a semitruck trailer stacked floor to ceiling with cages of feral cats. This was an entire subculture! While standing in line, I overheard conversations about wily ferals impossible to catch and new techniques tried, about how many were caught this week and how many they expected to catch next. These were your hard-core, cat tattoo–sporting veterans, who had worked the trenches before I had even seen my first cat. When I eavesdropped on their war stories, it became immediately apparent that my caregiving had been mere child's play in comparison. I would see these same faces time and again as I brought more cats from the colony to be neutered, and I found comfort in the camaraderie.

I was next. An assistant welcomed me and peeked under the cage's cover, seeing Baby Gray, who was growling deeply. I handed her my application, and she quickly made corrections to my entries. She crossed out "caliby" (a calico-tabby mix) and wrote "tortie." She crossed out "medium hair" and wrote "short hair." These people know their cats.

Then she placed a strip of masking tape with written code onto the cage and said, "You'll receive a call once she wakes up from the anesthesia. If everything looks okay to the doctor, you'll be able to pick her up late this afternoon."

"You mean I won't know if she's okay for eight hours?!" I blurted out.

A hush fell over the clinic. All activity stopped, all eyes on me. Then knowing smiles, everyone realizing I was a newbie.

Some people oppose TNR on the grounds that outdoor cats harm songbird populations. But according to Alley Cat Allies, a national advocacy organization dedicated to the protection and humane treatment of cats:

Decades of studies prove that when cats do hunt — which is not nearly as often as they scavenge — they much prefer a diet of rodents. Studies have shown cats to be far more efficient hunters when they sit and wait for prey — outside a rodent burrow, for example — than when they stalk and pounce, the way they approach birds. As opportunistic feeders, cats are more likely to go for your garbage or sit and wait to catch rodents than to take their chances chasing birds who can easily spot them and fly away.

In areas devoid of rodents and rabbits, cats do tend to prey on birds. But studies have determined that in this scenario, cats "almost always catch only old, sick or young specimens." Even the UK's Royal Society for the Protection of Birds states, "It is likely that most of the birds killed by cats would have died anyway from other causes before the next breeding season, so cats are unlikely to have a major impact on populations."

With respect to this heated issue, I don't profess to have any expertise whatsoever. I can only speak from my own experience. In twenty years, though birds frequented the trees behind our house, rarely did I see our cats take one down. I only saw evidence of a total of three birds killed. Given the size of the colony, I find this remarkable. I'm sure any domestic cat or two would take down at least that many birds in as much time as our entire colony did.

I've seen birds fly right at my cats, and I've observed birds in the leaves just above their heads and within reach. The cats just watch, without attempting to attack them. I've even seen birds alight on cats' heads as they would on branches when flitting from tree to tree, and the felines don't react. Kittens sometimes pretend to hunt, but when I approach, they give me a look like that of a kid driven to the prom by his mom — I've ruined everything.

I once saw Charlie feign a move toward a jay, and the jay never forgot it. For weeks afterward, that bird would hound Charlie. Anytime we couldn't find Charlie, all we needed to do was find the squawking jay. Below the bird would be Charlie, noticeably disturbed by all the noise.

The waiting area quickly filled up with every size, breed, and disposition of feral cat imaginable, and their caretakers, an equally diverse group. I pulled back the cover on Baby Gray's cage, and we made eye contact. I told her I'd be waiting for her, and she blinked quickly at me twice. Holding back tears, I exited the clinic, breathing deep. I started walking, anywhere, just to keep from pacing like an anxious parent.

Minutes moved like molasses, and I could swear the sun hadn't budged an inch in the sky, even though two hours had passed. At long last, I got the call. Baby Gray was ready to be picked up. What a relief! When I returned to take Baby Gray home, I gingerly moved her cage to my car, peeked inside before driving off, and saw her groggy with anesthesia. Once home, I kept her in a warm corner of the house overnight, with food and water, planning to release her back into the wild the next day, per instructions.

Well, she was not a happy girl the next morning. She sneered and hissed at me from the cage. Even after I released her outside, expecting her to run and hide until she had fully recuperated, she stood and hissed at me. And she didn't just hiss — she leered, giving me the evil eye. I've never seen a cat so visibly upset. She made it clear that I had ruined her life.

Since FixNation required reservations well in advance and I never knew when I might capture a cat, I also made appointments at the local Humane Society, which offered free feral-cat fixing. So with staggered appointments, I began the challenging endeavor of trying to capture every cat in the colony.

I feared the inevitable would happen, and it did. Once the colony smelled Baby Gray and examined her shaved belly, they knew something had happened that they wanted to avoid. And they knew I was the culprit. The colony now treated me as a pariah. Instead of moving toward me, they shied away when I approached. Whereas before they would rest at ease in my presence, they were now on edge, constantly casting a wary eye my way. I had worked years to gain their trust, and now I had turned on them.

But then something shifted dramatically for Baby Gray. From one day to the next, she became my new best friend and began a long-standing custom of bringing me presents that continues to this day. Repetitive calls in the distance indicate that a present is headed my way. I'll run to the window and watch her lug the item up the driveway before placing it at either the front or back door, depending on her mood. At times, the gift is too cumbersome for her to carry without a break, so she'll drop it and rest before continuing.

It's especially fun to watch her handle a towel. As it hangs from her mouth, she straddles it, inching forward, careful to keep each of her four paws from stepping on it. I have no idea where she finds them, but I've received slippers, children's toys, flowers, shoes, socks, a new pair of sheer pink panties, and a pair of bright-green shorts. She's even brought me chamois infant wear, crib toys, and mobiles that might hang above a cradle.

Did this wild cat actually enter someone's home and snag these from a baby? I've half-jokingly told myself I should put a kitty cam on her to see how she does it. And her gifts are seasonal. At Thanksgiving, she brings me plastic autumn leaves, placing them perfectly in the middle of the welcome mat. You could take a ruler and see that she placed them absolutely dead center. I receive Christmas ornaments in winter and Easter eggs in the spring.

Did she come to realize that removing the burden of reproduction was a blessing in disguise? Was she grateful? No way of knowing. Still, something did change in our relationship, for the better. Unfortunately, it had no influence on the others.

The next cat I snared was Caliby. She's a clever one. At first, she tiptoed over the cage's trigger, grabbed the savory fresh salmon I knew she couldn't resist, and ran out of the trap without it closing behind her. Shadow saw how easy this was and grabbed the remaining salmon and walked out, too. I realized I needed a better trigger. I propped the trap open with a water bottle that had a long string attached, then I baited the trap again and waited nearby quietly. There was Caliby again, inching her way into the trap for easy food. Not this time. One she was inside, I pulled the bottle, and the trap snapped shut. She spun around in the trap and pushed against its sides, moaning quietly.

She, too, was moved into the garage for the day. I noticed that once these cats knew they were trapped with no way out, they went into something like a hibernation. They remained quiet and unmoving. The next morning, I moved Caliby's cage to the trunk of my car and drove her to the Humane Society. There were no other feral-cat caregivers here, and I missed their camaraderie. However, an elderly woman with two Siberian huskies was seated next to me, and she scoffed when she saw me filling out paperwork for my cat.

"You a cat lover?"

"Yeah, I guess you could say that."

"Never knew a man who liked cats. Must be your wife's, huh?"

"Well, no."

"Somebody's got you whipped. Girlfriend?"

Where in the world did she learn a phrase like that? I didn't know how to respond.

"Loser," she snorted as she walked off, rubbing her dogs with pride.

I fished for a retort but then considered the possibility that she might be speaking to a larger issue — something more signifi-cant than dog lovers versus cat lovers. It was snobbery, to be sure, but perhaps based on some kernel of truth. Dogs are sometimes thought of as being more dependable and civilized because they are fully domesticated, while cats have a reputation for being a little closer to the wild. Which is why articles show up with titles like "Why Does Your Cat Love You...Sort Of?"

Dogs have a jump on cats in the domestication arena by thou-sands of years, which explains why there are four hundred rec-ognized dog breeds compared with fewer than fifty for cats. And while cat genome sequencing has revealed genetic mutations re-sulting in neuronal pathways that make cats less aggressive and willing to approach and interact with humans, genes from their days as wildcats (when they were still *Felis sylvestris*) remain in-tact, providing them their keen senses of eyesight and hearing, and of course their ability to hunt. Put a dog back into the wild, and their excellent sense of smell would be about their only asset. Most would likely not survive.

Some scientists go so far as to describe cats as "semidomes-ticated," though others would probably equate that with being half-pregnant. Still, I feel the dog owner's reaction had as its basis a fear of the wild in some form. What we can't control scares us. As Melinda Zeder, an archaeologist at the Smithsonian Institution, says, "I think what confuses people about cats is that they still carry some of the more aloof behaviors of their solitary wild progenitors. Sometimes they don't give a damn about you.... Unlike dogs they do not have to constantly please and satisfy our needs."

I handed my paperwork to the attendant at the front desk, who then instructed me to bring the cage into the facility. I went back to my car, opened my trunk, and the cage was empty. Where was Caliby?

I checked the lock, and it was still intact. I checked the sides, the top, the bottom, any part of the cage she might've escaped from, and found no evidence whatsoever that she could've gotten out. As my trunk was large and filled with books, towels, and a Boogie Board, there were lots of places for her to hide, if in fact she was still in there.

I hurried inside to explain the situation, and two attendants followed me to the car with large nets. I felt certain she was still in there. Where else could she be? They moved me out of the way, covered the open trunk with their nets, and began rustling around, moving the towels, peeking under the books. And there she was. But this was not a happy cat. She hissed and howled and snapped and clawed, but was soon curled up at the bottom of an oversized net, which one attendant closed off with his gloved hand. To this day, I have no idea how she pulled a Houdini and escaped that cage.

Next to be captured was Boots, for an appointment with Fix-Nation. The only way I could catch her was by withholding food until she became so hungry she was willing to enter the strange contraption to eat. Keeping Boots from eating was simple. She was easily the most nervous of the group, so one merely needed to look at her funny to keep her from eating. I felt especially bad for taking advantage of her skittishness. But my mantra through-out the process of catching the cats was "It's for the good of the colony."

Rain came down in torrents on the day Boots was fixed. I felt uneasy and worried more than usual, which is saying a lot. The day felt ominous. I didn't even care whether they were successful with the surgery; I just wanted her home. When the call finally came, thankfully there was nothing but good news.

Gumdrop greeted her at the door and licked her through the cage as she rested, spending the night with her by pressing her body against Boots's cage. The heavy rain flooded our garage, so I kept her inside by the garage door, near the kitchen. When I checked on her near midnight, she was obviously uncomfortable, and I soon realized she had been holding in her need to evacuate all this time. Until now. I've never before seen an embarrassed cat; this was as close as I was going to get. I apologized to her, that she had to experience this humiliation. Or maybe I was the one who was humiliated. But I felt we formed a bond at that moment that stayed with us for the rest of her life.

In the morning when she was released back outside, it was obvious Boots had lost the use of her back leg. I called the clinic and explained the situation. They asked if I would take a video on my phone showing her compromised ambulation and email it to them. No easy task. Boots, daughter of Outsider, was normally the last cat I could get close to. But perhaps because she was hurt and knew I was trying to help, she approached me with no trepi-dation whatsoever. Once I readied my cell phone, she turned her injured hind leg toward me, then walked away in slow motion, making sure I could see the problem. Had I not seen this myself, I never would've believed it. Then she turned back to look at me, as if asking if I got the shot, before limping away. She never got that close to me again for the rest of her life. I emailed the video to the clinic director, who showed it to the on-call vet. He had seen this before. Nerve damage that would correct itself in a matter of days, he opined. And he was right.

Though Gumdrop kept company with and nurtured many cats we had fixed, they certainly didn't return the favor. One day, soon after I began fixing the cats, I found Gumdrop abandoned on her side, breathing fast and shallow, obviously in shock. I approached cautiously, looking for evidence of an injury. She pushed herself to her feet, and when she did, her right arm dangled. I could then see she had dislocated her elbow.

This wasn't a great surprise. From the time she was a kitten, she had been a little bowlegged. Landing on her elbow funny, when jumping down from a high place, must have knocked the elbow from its socket. She gingerly followed me inside, hopping on her one good front leg, and gimped her way upstairs before diving onto Sophie's thick, soft quilt, the injured foot tucked beneath her for protection. Amazing how animals can adapt so quickly.

Time for a trip to Dr. V's.

Yet another cat to be added to the already large file they had on us. For a stoic guy, Dr. V sure showed his soft side when he saw Gumdrop for the first time. He gushed over her coloration and demeanor, her satin fur and crisp golden eyes. A heartbreaker for sure. After examining her, he didn't feel confident he could reset her elbow, due to her innate bowleggedness. He asked that she be kept at his clinic for a few days, on muscle relaxants, and he would see what he could do. Otherwise it would need to be surgically repaired, which he said would cost thousands. This wasn't good news.

Thankfully he was able to reset Gumdrop's arm. He wrapped it well, and after a few weeks, she seemed strong enough to go back outside again. We were careful to carry her down from high places whenever she was poised to jump. But months later, I found Gumdrop by the garbage cans on her side again, panting. Charlie was with her this time, uncharacteristically licking her. I was certain she had been hit by a car. Then I noticed that same elbow, again dislocated. I rushed her to Dr. V, who said he would give it one more try. He felt that if it didn't work this time, he would probably need to amputate the limb since she was just too active for surgery.

He kept her again for a few days and eventually was able to work her elbow back into place. This time, to ensure the elbow would heal completely, he created a very strong and complex wrap — which she tore apart with her teeth in less than an hour. When we showed up again at his office later the same day, he remarked that she was smarter than he was. He had attended vet school and spent years learning the best techniques, and here she had undone everything he had been taught, in less than an hour.

This time the repair took. Now, every evening when she is ready to come inside from her day out, she waits on top of the fence for us to carry her in, somehow knowing that by jumping down, she might reinjure her elbow. She has also assumed a new sleeping position. Every night, she sleeps over the weak arm, tucking it beneath her chin and pressing her head against the ground so nothing can bother the arm.

Not long after resolving Gumdrop's elbow problem, I spotted Charlie making his way to our front door late one night, hopping on three legs. Just what I needed! Studying him as he walked, I could see he was unable to put any pressure on his front left leg, and he was obviously in pain. A broken leg for such an active cat had "impossible" written all over it. I carried him inside and studied him carefully. I felt gently down the entire leg, checking to see if there was a spot that caused him more pain than anywhere else. I needed him immobile, so I put him inside our cat cage for the night and let him rest in the garage. When I described the situation to Stacey at Dr. V's the next morning, she said to bring him in immediately.

When I arrived, she gave me priority, bumping other appointments so Charlie could be seen quickly. Dr. V looked more serious than usual, feeling along Charlie's entire leg as I had the night before. He closed the door of the examination room and lifted Charlie from the table, placing him gently on the floor. Charlie suddenly started running around the room normally, putting weight on the arm without even a limp.

I turned beet red. "Char...lie!"

Dr. V laughed long and deep.

"I'm really so sorry. I thought it was broken."

"That's okay, that's okay. I still think it's something."

He lifted Charlie back onto the table and examined him again. Charlie winced when he pressed into the armpit.

"He was bit. Bee sting, maybe wasp. He'll be okay. It's okay."

I reprimanded Charlie all the way home. But he had already dozed off. Probably due to his fitful sleep in the cage the night before. He wasn't exactly sleeping; he was "purr sleeping." From the time Charlie was a kitten, he was such a happy cat that even when he slept, he purred.

Tiny was next in line for getting fixed. The thought of anything going wrong while she was under the knife kept the whole house sleepless. My housemates gave her a big hug on the day of her appointment and assured her we would see her later that day. Off we went. On the drive over, I sang her the familiar songs we had composed for her, though I was only pretending to be upbeat.

I took one last look at her before the attendant took her away, and I memorized the time on the clock. This would be the longest day of my life. I drove in circles around the FixNation facility so many times I was drawing stares from the neighbors. So I went to an adjacent neighborhood and drove circles there. I wanted to be nearby in case Tiny needed me. Obviously I was being a nuisance, so I parked near a vacant lot and just sat. And sat. I promised myself I wouldn't check the time every ten minutes, but I did.

Finally the long-awaited call. I closed my eyes, cringing as I answered. Those glorious words, "You can come pick up your cat. Everything went fine." Hallelujah. I called Sophie and Heather immediately to give them the good news before rushing over to pick her up. She was groggy from the anesthesia, but her eyes were open, and she was moving slightly.

I sang her songs all the way home. According to protocol, we kept her in the cage overnight, in the kitchen area. Gumdrop became her welcome committee, as usual, and licked her through the cage before stretching her body out against Tiny's to spend the night next to the cage.

Come morning, Tiny was obviously in pain and unsettled. I carried her upstairs and placed her on my bed. She sat next to me, then ever so slowly crawled her way under my arm, seeking protection. This she has done since a kitten, whenever in fear or needing my help. This time, she stayed glued to me, not letting me move without her moving with me, hiding under my arm the whole time. Having been introduced to opera, she used to like it when her favorite arias were being played. But they had no impact on her now.

I made a small hutch on my bed for her, right next to my pillow. She watched me construct the blue-flannel home and immediately knew that it was hers. She crawled inside and then pawed at me, not yet content. I placed my hand on her shaved belly, and then she could rest. Later that night, I realized she had carried every single one of her toys into her hutch, except for a toy opossum on a string that she managed to get only halfway in. For the next three weeks, she wouldn't leave that hutch except when hungry or needing to relieve herself. But she had to hurry back as fast as possible, to curl up under its protection again and rest. And she couldn't sleep unless my hand stayed on her belly (which was sewn with dissolvable stitches) through the night. This routine lasted for three weeks. And then one day, she never entered the hutch again, so I dismantled it.

Given the challenges Tiny had experienced in her life, we weren't surprised that of all the cats we fixed, she was the only one with a lingering complication — ovarian remnant syndrome. It's likely that a piece of ovarian tissue was left inside her during her surgery. As a result, at times she becomes noticeably uncomfortable and vocal. The only remedy is to have that piece of tissue removed. Dr. V decided against it, feeling the risks of a second surgery were too great. He said sometimes accessory ovarian tissue can separate from the main ovary and remain hidden in the abdominal wall. So even if the cat is spayed successfully, the surgeon might not see the remnant of ovarian tissue. As worked up as she's always tended to get, she now gets doubly so — several times a month!

Three sisters enjoying the view out the window.

13 Three Sisters

M onths passed, and the cats were becoming more and more difficult to trap. But none could resist pangs of hunger from my withholding their food, combined with a trick I learned from savvy caregivers I met at FixNation: Kentucky Fried Chicken, Original Recipe. Tie a single drumstick to the back of the cage, and I went from leper to matinee idol. Now I had to shoo cats away, to keep several from ending up in the trap at the same time.

The last holdout was Snow White. She ran at the sight of me, KFC drumstick or not. We were in no hurry. She was pregnant, and we decided hers would be the colony's last litter. I made a point of feeding her the best canned food I could find, to make sure she was well nourished. Once she disappeared to birth her kittens, we didn't see her again until she was famished. She would show up in our backyard and, if food wasn't there, immediately run back to her kittens, without waiting. I made sure I was always ready with food for her.

Finally came the day she showed off her litter to us. She carried them one by one by the neck, and placed them gently on the back side of the fence in a nest of grass. There they would be safe. But Snow White stayed on our side of the fence. So one day, these little kittens inched their way under the fence and straggled over to be reunited with their mother and nurse on her, and that's when we saw them clearly for the first time. There were two tuxedos (cats of black and white color), a white tabby, and a dark tortie. We complimented Snow White on her lovely litter, which we were now tasked with keeping safe. Thankfully it would be the last time we had to protect a litter of kittens.

That night, there was an attack, and the dark tortie was killed. The following afternoon, we watched Snow White's remaining kittens eating food with other colony cats. One of the tuxedo cats looked at us with beautiful green eyes and wouldn't look away. It held our gaze, and we were mesmerized.

I stated the obvious to my housemates: "You know we won't be able to keep them safe."

They nodded.

"What do you want to do?"

"Bring them inside."

"Are you sure?"

The sisters looked at each other a long time.

"Yes."

We all knew what that meant. A lifetime commitment.

I crouched outside as the kittens were eating, and poised my hands under the two tuxedo cats, who were several weeks old.

I turned back to the sisters, who were waiting at the back door, one last time. "Are you sure?"

They nodded and held the door wide open. Whoosh, I swept the two tuxedos into the house. They slid along the slick tile floor before scurrying under the couch. But not before giving me good scratches and bites, which amazed me, given how small they were. Feral to the bone. And the larger of the two let off a stink bomb unlike anything I had ever smelled. It saturated the house like skunk spray, lasting for days. Even Tiny cringed at the stench. I later learned some cats release fluid from their anal sac glands when frightened, and that's what we were smelling.

That left the little chubby white tabby. A beauty. I was particularly determined to catch this one, given our poor track record with white cats. It shied away from me after seeing what I had done with its littermates. So I prepared the trapping cage, placing food at one end and propping up the cage door with a plastic water bottle with string attached.

This kitten had never seen a cage before. Curious, it entered the contraption cautiously and moved toward the food. I yanked the bottle by the string, and the cage door slammed shut. Easy catch. I carried the cage into the house and opened the cage door, but the kitten wouldn't come out. So I reached in and pried its small paws from the cage sides it was gripping, and plop — onto the tile floor. This cutie immediately scurried away behind the couch, too.

For weeks on end, they stayed hidden. Their mother, Snow White, seemed at ease. She never called for them as she had for previous litters. And she could watch them through our screen door. When the kittens got older and we would take them outside on leashes, she would visit them for short periods of time and then walk away, seemingly satisfied that her brood was in good hands. We placed both dried and canned kitten food in bowls close to the couch where they lived, and provided several litter boxes they could choose from. Two of them caught on to the litter boxes right away. But one did not. We're not sure who. We even bribed them to tell us, but they wouldn't sing.

At any given time of day or night, we'd hear the scamper of little feet, the chomping of food, the scattering of cat litter. Then they'd rush back behind the couch. If we happened to be sitting on the couch, Sophie would often say, "There are bugaboos right under us!"

Over time, their appearances lasted longer. They would hide under our glass table, between the glass itself and a metal-mesh support a few inches below, which gave them a sense of protection. But of course they were in plain view under the glass. We set up several boxes they would all crawl into, but they still didn't want to be handled. And still don't, to this day.

The reason they came out of hiding was Charlie, our orange tabby alpha male. For some reason, all three kittens immediately bonded with him as if he were their mother. Whenever he came into the house, they would squeal with delight, run to him, cuddle, and even try to nurse on him. To this day, that relationship hasn't changed. They brought out his soft side, and we often see him licking the kittens and caring for them as a mother might.

Soon after he established a relationship with the kittens, I found Charlie lying in an unusual place upstairs. The light in his eyes was dim, and I was worried. I knew immediately we had a dangerously sick cat on our hands. He was so ill I imagined I'd never see him well again. I felt that whatever he had might kill him.

Dr. V thought so, too. After determining that Charlie had a 108-degree fever, he rushed Charlie to the ICU and put him on IVs. Charlie stayed sick for five days, but Dr. V kept at it, trying a different antibiotic cocktail every twelve hours until, miraculously, he happened on the right formula. Finally Charlie's fever broke. When at last I could bring him home, I crammed the bill on my over-the-limit credit card, after pleading with the bank. Though he was skinny at first and it took time for him to convalesce, I eventually began to see the old Charlie again. He seemed to experience no residual trauma from his illness. As always, he was a very present cat, just responding to what was happening now, as if the past didn't exist.

But unfortunately whatever virus he'd had was passed along to all three kittens. I rushed them all to Dr. V's office, and people in the waiting room hurried over to look, oohing and aahing at the cuteness of these kittens. I beamed as if I had given birth to them myself.

Stacey reached for one cat, asking, "Do they have names?"

I nodded.

"How about this one?"

"We named him Bandit."

She turned the cat over and said, "Maybe not. You've got a girl here."

"Really?" (We changed her name to Bandy.)

"Really."

"And this one?"

"Pierre."

"Pierre?"

"He looked French to me. See his angular face and European sensibilities?"

"No."

I pointed to the curved white mark on his forehead that was identical to the logo of a French cosmetics company, and said, "See the Sephora logo on his forehead?"

She studied the mark before turning the cat over. "Sorry, you've got another girl here."

My jaw dropped.

She reached for the third kitten. "And look at this precious white tabby."

"Cozy."

"Well, Cozy could go for either sex, so I think you're okay." Turning the cat over, she said, "Another girl. You've got three sisters."

Their fevers were as high as Charlie's had been, so they, too, spent many nights in the animal hospital before being cured of the virus. The single virus that hit Charlie and the sisters caused me so much financial pain, I considered insuring them with Lloyd's of London.

Still, it wasn't as expensive as it could have been. Dr. V once again gave us a generous discount on what would otherwise have been a prohibitively expensive bill. I only wish I could have thanked him again. For his help in this crisis, and every other crisis we brought him. He died soon after. A trusted, loving member of our family gone. We were certain we wouldn't be able to replace him, and we were right.

We called the three sisters the Cutesies. For some reason, they never seemed to grow out of their kitten phase, and even today Sophie refers to them as the Diaper Pack. As time went by, the two tuxedo cats seemed to know they shared similar markings and would nuzzle together quietly for hours on end. When they did, we called them the Oreo Cookies. The white tabby seemed to sense she was different and stayed alone, often nuzzling up to one of our shoes. This was clearly an example of two males impregnating the same cat.

We had never seen a male matching Cozy's coloration. Until several months later, when a large, male white tabby, whom Cozy happened to spot, came to our back door. She ran to the door, and they smelled each other through the mesh screen, obviously kin. At last, someone she could relate to! Another example of a male coming to check on his brood. I was told by a feral-cat trapper at FixNation that a male does this by smell. Scent markings enable a male to recognize and locate his offspring.

Once they were about six months old and had put on some weight, it was time to have the three sisters spayed. Prior to that, however, we attempted to have their mother, Snow White, fixed. That turned out to be no easy task. She stayed wary of me, remaining impossible to catch. But I was driven by a strong incentive: she was the last colony member who could become impregnated, and I just couldn't live through another batch of kittens.

So I purchased a plastic laundry basket and a large piece of heavy cardboard. I cut out the cardboard to match the size of the laundry basket mouth exactly. Then I took the basket outside, which of course made all the cats nervous. I pulled up a chair and during every feeding held the laundry basket above the cats. They eventually became so hungry they didn't care what I held over their heads.

After more than a week of this ritual, the cats adapted. "That stupid guy is going to be out there again with his chair and laundry basket. Who cares?" But just as Snow White stopped paying any attention to me, *whoomp!* I dropped the basket over her body. I called for Sophie to hold the basket firm while I hurried inside for the cardboard I had cut. I slid the cardboard under the basket, then began wrapping the entire contraption with clear packing tape, in endless circles, until it was secure.

I placed the basket with Snow White inside in the garage, then cut away a piece of the basket and slid a water bowl inside for her, before taping up the hole again. Unlike any cat I had ensnared in the past, she didn't make a sound. Not a single peep. I drove her to FixNation the next day, still marveling at her silence but even more impressed by her presence. She felt incredibly powerful, a force of nature, and frankly I felt grateful to be with her like this, in such proximity.

When I carried the laundry basket into FixNation with Snow White inside, other feral caregivers came around, excited, saying they had heard you could capture difficult cats this way, yet no one had ever seen it. But the attendants weren't amused. I hadn't followed protocol, and they weren't going to accept the cat. Apparently when you use this method, you must secure the basket to the base with screws and bolts. Tape was not strong enough and could put the doctors at risk. I could see they were right. But no way in hell was I going to take this cat home. So the attendants were kind enough to bring out screws and bolts they had on hand and secure the basket to the cardboard. She was accepted.

Now it was time to fix her daughters, the three sisters. I realized this would be my last trip to FixNation, and it was a bittersweet realization. At one point, the colony had numbered more than fifty cats. And after nature thinned the herd over time, I was tasked with overseeing the spaying or neutering of more than a dozen cats. Now I'd be seeing my fellow feral-cat caregivers, and the office staff, doctors, and clinic manager, for the last time.

It didn't seem to matter that I had been through this routine many times; it always felt like the first time. Had I been a smoker, I would've gone through a carton by the time they were done. By late afternoon, I received the call. No other life experience evoked both hope and fear simultaneously as much as that afternoon call. I was going to be told either that my cats were ready to be picked up or that they didn't make it.

A sigh of relief. The Cutesies had all awakened from their anesthesia and were ready to go home. I bid a teary farewell to those at the clinic and closed the doors behind me for the last time.

As I drove slowly home, I reflected on the amount of anguish these trips to the clinic had caused me. I realized I had basically been holding my breath for all the months it took to get every cat fixed, and I had yet to exhale. Still, we hadn't lost one cat to the procedure. Not even a severe complication.

I wondered what else terrified me in life that would never come to pass. Phantoms of fear having their origin in who knows what.

One of the ancient Hindu scriptures, the Mandukya Upanishad, speaks to delusion and misconception as the cause of fear, by describing a villager who approached a well and became terrified at mistaking a coiled rope for a large snake ready to strike. She was certain she was about to be bitten and die. It wasn't until an old man came to the well and told her she was confusing the rope for a snake that she realized her mistake.

Shakespeare may have put it most succinctly:

Cowards die many times before their deaths;
The valiant never taste of death but once.

Ah, now that the three sisters had overcome their viruses and been spayed, all was right with the world again. Until the fleas. Our home became infested with them. They wreaked havoc on the Cutesies, especially Bandy. She was covered with sores, and her distress was obviously stunting her growth. Her sisters grew appropriately, but she did not. But Sophie suffered more from the fleas than the cats did. Her entire body was covered in bites. We researched the most thorough and nontoxic remedy for fleas and decided Borax was our best bet. We coated the entire house with the powder and then waited a day before vacuuming everything up. In just one treatment, we rid the entire house of fleas and have never had a single recurrence since.

But Bandy still ailed. It was more from scratching her sores than from fleas at this point, as she would scratch and open new wounds. She looked like a horror kitty during Halloween. That's when I discovered a product called Soft Paws. These are soft plastic nail covers secured by a nontoxic adhesive, so if a cat chews them off, there are no ill effects. As often happened when I came up with ideas for the cats, my housemates laughed at me. I admit many of my schemes were far-fetched.

Gluing plastic nail covers onto a feral kitten is no easy feat. But just two days after we started using Soft Paws (which are offered in a myriad of colors, by the way), Bandy's wounds cleared up, and she was in fine spirits again, eating voraciously. My housemates were amazed. Every few days, I would find a discarded nail cover on the ground and need to attach a new one. Let's try a pink one this time. How about green? Bandy was the talk of the town, looking quite fashionable in her color-coordinated "nail polish."

Once again peace had returned to the household. I came to relish those little respites. It was never a question of whether there would be another crisis; it was a question of when. And in this case, it came almost immediately.

Little Pierre scurried out the front door one evening, surprising even herself. There she sat, crouched by the front door, unsure of her next move. Sophie sat just inside the house, her hand reaching gently toward Pierre, explaining to Pierre in soft tones why she really needed to come back inside. Pierre seemed torn. Sophie was almost reaching her now, any part of her small body would do. But Pierre bolted.

Days passed, and we didn't see her. Then a week. She was gone. The unspoken understanding in our now solemn house was that she was just too small and naive to survive. Our only chance was that Animal Control or a neighbor might have picked her up, so I spent hours on end poring over photos of recently captured cats on Animal Control and Humane Society websites.

Eventually I thought I spotted a cat online that looked familiar. It was at a shelter ten miles away. This cat had the same

Sephora mark on her forehead, and I was cautiously optimistic. Then I pulled up a photo I had of Pierre on my computer and enlarged both, and was saddened to realize their marks didn't match exactly.

Another sorrowful week passed. Bandy slept alone now, without her twin to comfort her. Cozy didn't seem to realize anyone was missing. By week three, we didn't mention Pierre again, except for the occasional comment by Sophie, lamenting the fact that she had been inches from rescuing her. If only she had lunged at her.

Late one night, I decided to go for a drive and walked out to my car, which was parked on the street. The chill in the air made me realize I didn't have a heavy enough coat on, so I turned around to walk back to the house. I was halfway there when out of the small shrub we shared with our neighbor came Caliby to greet me. My radar went up because neither Caliby nor any of the ferals ever greeted me. And right behind her was a small black cat with white markings.

"You've gotta be kitten me," I said aloud. "It can't be."

And then I noticed the Sephora mark on her forehead and tried to calm myself so as not to frighten her off. But there was no chance of that, for as soon as Pierre saw me, she made small chirping sounds and spun around in circles, seemingly as happy to see me as I was to see her.

Caliby ran for the backyard, and little Pierre followed her. I hurried inside, yelling as loud as I could, "Pierre sighting! Pierre sighting!" I ran to the back door and promptly put out food. It seemed Pierre had bonded with her stepsister Caliby while outside, so whatever Caliby did, she followed. Seeing Caliby eating, she ate, too.

I screamed back in the house, "Pierre!" Finally Sophie and Heather came running downstairs. I found out later they both thought I was joking. And Sophie took it further, telling me she had been muttering to herself upstairs, and I quote, "Stupid, stupid, dummy. Why would he joke about something like that?" But, in fact, there Pierre was. It was a miracle that she'd stayed safe and somewhat nourished all that time. As she gobbled her food, I crept out, grabbed her tightly, and tossed her inside, just like the day I brought her indoors for the first time.

She was very thin, but certainly not as emaciated as she would have been if she hadn't eaten at all. Stacey at the vet's office didn't have much to suggest except giving her small amounts of canned food many times a day along with dried, for now. And bringing her in if complications arose.

My housemates and I couldn't help but use the word *miracle* to describe Pierre's returning to us. I'm not sure what makes miracles happen. I've heard you can attract them by "expecting" one. I've seen things I would consider miraculous. An explosion of brilliant light suddenly descending from a Mother Mary statue onto a devout worshipper (I even have photos). The light of a person's soul streaking across the sky at the moment of their death. Rainbows lighting up the sky on a cloudless day during a great lama's cremation. I've seen multicolored snake deities rise from a shallow pond of water and nectar pour from a goddess that self-manifested from solid rock. I've seen hand- and footprints of saints pressed into granite and a lama dematerialize in front of my face.

But I've also seen the maligned forgive, and the sun rise. I've marveled at the color of a peacock and the intricacies of a fly's wings and a person's smile. At the miracle of a gentle touch or a kind nod of the head. All while racing around the Sun at more than 65,000 mph, while our solar system circles the center of our galaxy at more than 500,000 mph. Perhaps the word *miraculous* could be used for just about everything. Even seemingly horrible things. Maybe there's an intelligence to it all.

Marble enjoying a snack.

14 Indoors and Out

Feral cats we hand-raised, like Charlie, Gumdrop, and Tiny, learned to naturally come and go from the house. That's not to say their presence inside was not without its challenges. The first casualties were our window screens. Their sharp nails pierced them like flame throwers through cotton candy. We even caught a few jailbreaks — cats climbing through screens they had decimated before they were old enough to be allowed outside. One, who shall remain nameless, was even caught halfway out, her body straddling the window frame. But I have no qualms about naming the leader of their escape: it was Charlie.

I was forced to order custom screens made of a claw-resistant material. Because, I rationalized, how can you have cats indoors without making open windowsills and outdoor breezes available for them? The screens weren't cheap, but I discovered that nothing was cheap with cats. Nothing. Except the Borax for the fleas. Two bucks.

Unlike our other cats, who learned to come and go, the Cutesies did not. As they got older, we experimented with letting them out, but they went completely wild almost immediately. I want to say they "went native," but I don't think that's politically correct, though it captures the feeling better. Going back to nature. You could actually observe it in their faces after about ten minutes. Like they'd never seen you before. Your lover with their arms around another man or woman, except that their suitor was nature.

At first, I felt unappreciated. Perhaps as a parent might after exerting tremendous effort raising a child, only to be scorned by them during a rebellious adolescence. And that's when I had to remind myself that these were wild animals and that I was to expect no reciprocity. But still...

When one of the three sisters was outside and wouldn't return on her own, Sophie was the go-to person. She'd hear me knocking on her door late at night and know it was for a cat rescue. She would calmly go outside in the middle of the night, assess the situation, and come up with a plan. It usually consisted of one of us herding the AWOL cat around to one side of the house while the other blocked the other side, leaving the wide open back door as the only option. Should a cat decide to leap for the fence instead, we were ready for that, too.

A year after her miraculous rescue, Pierre escaped again, and within a matter of minutes turned wild. We saw her hiding in various places in the deep underbrush and amid machinery our neighbors stored at the side of their house. At least she was staying nearby. What worried us, however, was that she wasn't nourishing herself. We would occasionally see her eating a few kernels of kibbles with the rest of the colony outside, but not enough to sustain herself. She became weaker and weaker as the days passed, but still wouldn't let us capture her. Had she been caring for herself, we probably would've left her outside for good.

One day, I'd had enough. I was going to catch her no matter what. As I strode defiantly along the side of the house, I walked past a cat sleeping on the fence who I didn't realize was Pierre until I had passed her. As I looked back, there she was, skinny and deep asleep, wedged on top of the fence between a slat and a post so she wouldn't fall. Without a second thought, I grabbed her by the scruff of the neck with one hand and by the top of her back with the other, and raced around the corner, kicking open the door and sliding her inside. I yelled "Pierre's home!" and everyone came running this time, ecstatic.

As the saying goes, a parent is only as happy as their least happy child. Whenever one of our cats was outside or otherwise unaccounted for, my housemates and I remained in a constant state of unease. We couldn't focus at work; we couldn't sleep. Beneath our casual conversations would fester the dread that we were missing a cat.

Several years later, Pierre escaped once more. By this time, she had grown into a large, strikingly beautiful cat. Very strong and powerful, but also sublime and graceful. While out, she slept in a rusted-out generator at the side of the house and, again, wasn't eating. As usual, she didn't recognize us at all soon after escaping. But this time her reaction was even more extreme. She would run from the very sight of us. A first. She even shimmied up the fence once, leaping into the tree and jumping more than twenty feet into the neighbor's yard to avoid us.

Seeing how malnourished she was becoming, and confident I couldn't catch her either by myself or with Sophie's help, I decided to call a professional animal control service. The various companies I contacted didn't think they could help. They could only guarantee capture in an enclosed environment, like an attic or basement. And nobody could come out for another week or so anyway.

Enough. I put on a heavy jacket and gloves, climbed over the machinery at the side of the house, and grabbed for her, but she evaded me, hiding under the neighbor's car. We were both exhausted from this game. She lay on her side. I did the same, sprawling on the ground alongside the car, looking at her.

"It's time to go inside now. We didn't raise you to live in rusty machinery."

She blinked her eyes, tiredly.

"You're a refined woman. Come back to where you belong."

I had observed in days prior, when we would try to catch her, the first thing she would do was lead with her tail. She had quite a lot of heft, so it was probably in flinging her tail out first that she maintained her balance and best prepared for escape. As I continued speaking to her, I gently moved one hand close to her tail. Then, while she continued to rest, I went for the scruff of her neck with my other hand. She reacted as expected, pulling her head from me. But her tail whipped backward, as I had also seen before — backward and right into my hand. I had her! And I wasn't letting go, no matter how much she injured me.

I gently pulled her by the tail from under the car, and once she was clear, supported her back with my other hand, to protect her tail from injury. She was a spinning ball of feral madness, ripping to shreds my jacket, shirt, and gloves. I was dripping blood, but I wasn't letting go. I kicked open the front door and inside she went. As soon as I washed all the blood from my hands, I texted my housemates, and once again there was great relief all around.

That night, all I could think of was: What if she hadn't whipped out her tail? What if we never caught her and she starved outside? What if I hadn't seen her on the fence the last time she escaped?

What if I hadn't been by those bushes the first time she escaped as a kitten? Since so many of our stories ended in tragedy, those with joyful endings were greatly appreciated. (We would later come to learn that Pierre suffered chronically from a flea allergy, which caused her to run away and act irrationally. Once she was treated for that condition she didn't feel the need to escape from us again.)

Pierre's sister Cozy grew into a strong, healthy cat. We marveled when she began to shed her baby fat and her feline swayback appeared. It must have been hidden under all that cushion. But then she became unable to keep food down. This occasionally happens with cats, but a chronic condition needs intervention. A vet from the twenty-four-hour animal hospital that saved Tiny's life knows me as a nervous mother. So besides Cozy's inability to keep food down, when she stopped urinating, too, the vet agreed to see me immediately, even though it was after midnight. It's rare that a female cat has urine blockages. That's mainly a concern for males. Stones or crystals can block their urethra, bringing about a serious condition that needs immediate medical attention.

The vet examined Cozy and gave her a urine test. She determined that the issue was just an anomaly and her inability to keep food down was due to a sensitive digestive system rather than anything more serious. She prescribed a special cat food, which we tried for a while and which seemed to work. I couldn't afford the prescription after a few weeks; so I tried an over-the-counter cat food with protein designed specifically for sensitive systems, and she held that down. My housemates tease me about how much I dote on Cozy. They say that even if she hiccups, I'll run to the vet at three in the morning. And they might be right.

It came as no surprise to my commodity brokers that the thousand dollars I wired into my account to trade with was gone in a matter of seconds. As if it had spontaneously combusted. I could just as well have taken "one large" (as they call a thousand bucks in the movies) and flushed it down the toilet, bypassing all the pretending-to-be-a-trader stuff. When money evaporates that quickly, there is a tendency to imagine what better use might have been made of it. Besides paying rent for starters, how about giving to the needy, the hungry, the cold? The only way I could rationalize the loss was by reminding myself it was for the cats. Since I held highly leveraged positions, had the trades worked out, the upside could have been just as sweet as the loss was painful. My screenwriting career was stillborn, and my days as an astrologer were numbered — though I was offered a book deal by a prominent publisher for a book on astrology, a result of what I imagined must have been a liquid lunch consisting of too many cosmopolitans between a New York City literary agent and the editor. Because who makes generous offers for books sight unseen anyway, without a book proposal or even a chat on the phone?

In any case, the book advance quickly got gobbled up paying down debt, and I had no other money coming in and lots going out. My expenses were greater than any salary I could hope to earn from any nine-to-five job for which I might be qualified. Granted, it was a pretty short list. I used to wake up in terror at the prospect that I was just a feline high fever or clogged urethra away from bankruptcy. I could always go back to living in my car. But now I had cats.

I decided my best option at this point was to fall back on dealing in antique Asian art, something I had begun doing in the mid-1980s but had given up. I left the business for two reasons. One, items were showing up with dubious provenance, making it more likely they were stolen or otherwise obtained in unsavory ways. The other had to do with the remarkable quality of fakes.

I once had a set of eighteenth-century golden mongooses that hadn't been offered in years. I presented them to a client in Asia who, the next day, sent me images of four sets of golden mongooses identical to the ones I had sent him. Exact replicas. So rare were the iconography and workmanship of these pieces that, in years spent dealing in art of this type, I had never come across anything like them before. Yet now I was sent four identical sets. Precise, down to the worn marks on the hind quarters and elbows. The same happened with a rare set of sandalwood skeletons I was offered. Six identical sets showed up in Hong Kong not a week later.

I decided that unless a piece could be traced to an important collection, had a history of auction records from a reputable house, or otherwise had a strong provenance, I had no interest in being involved. This sentiment was shared by a friend of mine who once worked for a major auction house. She was considered extremely knowledgeable in her field and had worked for many years preparing pieces of important Asian art for auction. One day while she was prepping a piece, it slipped from her hands and broke on the floor. Frantic, she carefully examined the broken statue, only to realize it was a fake. She quit the same day. If fakes had become so good even the experts were fooled, she wanted no part of it.

I made contact with my old Asian art–dealing cronies, who were happy to hear from me. People buying and selling antique Asian art are a somewhat small and incestuous group, so new blood is always welcome, as long as you're known within the network. It offers both the possibility of new clients and the potential for fresh material.

The business had certainly changed since I was last involved. What used to entail meeting clients in person with the piece in hand or viewing pieces at archival storage facilities was all now facilitated by phone and computer. Amazingly, since getting back into the business, I have yet to meet a single client in person; nor has any buyer I've sold to viewed the piece prior to purchase. And there've been no complaints.

The phone/internet system of art dealing does have one drawback. It's nearly impossible to keep a piece confidential. Images can instantly show up on computers in Europe and Asia with a flick of the Forward button. You know instantly this has happened when the response is, "This piece is burned. Everyone already knows about it." (A "burned" piece is one that will never sell.) This has little to do with how significant a piece may be and everything to do with the impression that it's not unique if everyone already knows about it. No matter how wonderful the piece might be.

The stigma of being a burned piece is nearly impossible to overcome. That's why many sellers forgo auctions, since if a piece doesn't sell, not only has it been exposed, but it now has a history of not selling. It doesn't matter if the piece was offered at the wrong auction, or the reserve was set too high, or any other number of excuses the owner or owner's agent will give — the piece is likely burned.

A friend sent me an image of a collectible piece of antique Asian art he photographed atop his kitchen counter one afternoon. He asked that I not send it around, as he wanted to keep it quiet. That evening, I received the very same image from multiple contacts around the world, asking if I would be interested in the piece. My friend was dumbfounded. He couldn't believe the piece had already circulated. When he pressed me to make sure it was the same image, I said, "Do you have a box of corn flakes in the left corner of your counter?" And he did.

Dealing in Asian art again, I began making the cost of a month of cat expenses a day. Everything got figured in terms of cats. How much did you make today? Enough for a vet visit? A generalist appointment or a specialist? Did you make enough for a few days in the animal ICU?

Then, just as I was hitting my stride, the stock market crash in China caused many collectors to liquidate their collections in order to free up funds. Suddenly the market was flooded with valuable pieces of antique Asian art being offered at rock-bottom prices. I just couldn't compete with that.

I have since segued into brokering the occasional piece of fine art and am currently involved with a priceless Russian reliquary coffer. And I still have an idea for a commodity trade the cats and I could retire on. And I'm developing several TV pilots that seem promising. Or we'll be "living in a van down by the river." Hope springs eternal.

While our focus had been mainly on the three sisters at the time, drama always showed up where it was least expected. Beige appeared one evening with a growth on the side of his head. I couldn't tell if this was a tumor or an abscess, but it looked nasty. As days passed, he was having a harder and harder time eating, and his overall demeanor had changed to indicate he truly was suffering. I tried to capture him in a cage so he could be seen by the vet, but he would have none of that. And since he had a flagging appetite, coaxing him into the cage with food wasn't going to work. I called a neighborhood vet and asked if he'd be willing to prescribe a general antibiotic for him, sight unseen. After hearing the details of my predicament, he agreed. I mixed the small amount of liquid antibiotic he gave me with a teaspoon of canned food, just about the amount Beige could manage to eat, and within a few days, the abscesses burst. Two weeks later, as his appetite increased and we could add the full dose of antibiotics to his food, the oozing infection reduced to nothing, until there was no sign of the injury at all.

Soon after, a very unusual-looking male cat wandered into our backyard. Was he truly a cat or some type of hybrid laboratory experiment that had escaped? From his shoulders up to his brindled head, perky ears, and green eyes, he looked normal.

But from his shoulders down, he looked like a hyena, with a wide crimson stripe down the middle of his back, accented with spots on his sides. And he moved in a swaying hunchback fashion, like a wild animal.

Of course we called him Hyena. Or more accurately Ena, since when we greeted him, we'd say, "Hi, Ena." He was obviously suffering from mange, so I didn't want him mixing with our colony. But Sophie took an instant liking to him and felt he had made his way to us because he had nowhere else to go. She committed herself to caring for him, starting by training him to eat his food in his own special spot, away from the other cats. There he sat, not moving, until she brought him his food, which she did twice a day. He would look up at her through his mangy scabs and knotted hair, and softly bat his eyes at her in thanks.

After eating, he would disappear deep in the bushes to rest. The colony cats were completely apathetic toward him, as if he were a rock or a fallen pinecone. No reaction whatsoever. Over time, he gained some of his strength back and began grooming himself. A big job indeed.

He suffered a setback during a particularly violent rainstorm that lasted several days. His mange returned with a vengeance, and he was further hampered by difficulty walking, as if his lower back or hind legs had been injured. Since he was impossible to catch, I couldn't have him seen by a vet. But I felt antibiotics would help. We had some broad-spectrum liquid antibiotics left over from Beige's ordeal and began mixing it into his canned food, twice daily.

After a few weeks, though he had lost most of his hair, a new thick coat of hair began to grow in, and soon he was covered in a soft, downy pelt. He was still weak, but his spirits seemed to improve. Instead of being constantly nervous and scared, he softened. He knew we were caring for him and seemed to find deep comfort in that.

A week later, another male made an appearance. A hyperaggressive tabby we called Orange Crush. Ena was just finishing up his canned food when Crush lunged at him, grabbing him by the neck in a death grip. This wasn't a male trying to scare away another male; this was a fight to the death. I ran at them hissing, expecting that my presence would be enough to make them scatter. But there was no response. Ena's neck firmly lodged in Crush's mouth now, I kicked Orange Crush in order to save Ena's life, but he didn't seem to feel it. Seeing Ena fading now, I hauled off and kicked Crush as hard as I could with my bare feet, sending both cats flying into the air. They landed on a blue terra-cotta flowerpot that shattered on impact. With that, Crush released his grip and ran away, as did Ena.

Later, I spotted Ena lying in the driveway. I approached cautiously, trying to gauge how severe his injuries might be. His head perked up and he looked my way, but he didn't move. So I came close, studied his neck, and didn't see anything that might be lasting damage. He appeared at dinnertime as usual, not seeming too worse for wear, considering what he'd been through.

That wasn't the last we saw of Orange Crush. Days later, Cozy was outside on her leash, resting in her nest on the other side of the fence, when through the fence slats, she spotted an orange cat walking by. Certain it was Charlie, she crawled under the fence and ran to him with excited cries. Crush whipped around and sneered at her. She stopped in shock, having never before seen a cat that looked like Charlie but wasn't.

Later that day, from inside the house, I saw Charlie come tearing around the corner into the backyard, obviously scared. Behind him ran Orange Crush, charging at full speed. Before I knew it, Crush was standing over Charlie's prone body, ready to attack. I had never seen another cat threaten Charlie's domain or position as an alpha male and was surprised at his reaction. He just lay on his side, his stomach exposed submissively, cowering for the inevitable attack without even trying to defend himself. I stepped outside and had a stern talk with Crush. And then I had a talk with Charlie about needing to defend himself. When I told Sophie what I had seen, she blamed me for not teaching my boy how to fight.

Though we couldn't trust the sisters to be outside on their own, it was clear they needed fresh air and exercise. I bought them body harnesses, to which I attached a long, colorful yellow-and-blue nylon rope, measured perfectly for each cat. Cozy, in her pink body harness, would be able to reach the nest of her birth, just under the fence, where she loved to sit. Bandy, in a purple harness, would have just enough rope to sit in her favorite tree fort, an old-growth stump buried under ancient fronds. And Pierre, in her green harness, could slither through the bushes and spy on the neighbors and their dogs, as she tended to do.

I would take the sisters outside several times a day and night this way. The first thing each cat would do once outside was rub her body in the dirt, over and over again, rolling in it, coating her rich fur and colorful body harness a nice dusty brown. Clearly nature nourishes these cats in a way we can't.

A friend of mine had a pet cat he kept indoors its entire life, to protect it from the coyotes and bobcats that ran rampant in his neighborhood. When the cat was middle-aged and ill with cancerous tumors, my friend decided to let the cat outside, as he had always showed an interest in being outdoors. My friend installed a cat door and let him go. He also kept his garage door cracked, in case the cat needed to get inside in a hurry from the front yard. The experiment worked. Not only did the cat somehow stay safe, but spending the time outside seemed to enhance his health. In a matter of months, the tumors completely disappeared on their own. He went from being on his deathbed to living another eight years.

Not that his life outdoors was without drama. On several occasions, the cat would race into the house, an animal's body slamming against the garage door with a large thud right behind him. And at times, neighbors would call my friend, saying they had spotted a coyote tracking his cat. Still, he felt the benefits to his cat were worth the risks.

Sophie began having recurring dreams about Bandy. Horrible dreams of her being attacked by predators or otherwise running into some misfortune. She made me swear — not once, but many times — that whatever I did, I needed to protect Bandy at all costs. I don't know how many times I promised to keep her safe, but on the day she did run into trouble, I reacted instantly. Maybe that's why a parent drums a lesson into a child's head over and over again — so when the time comes to respond, it will be second nature.

Bandy was leashed and climbing in the trees under my supervision. But somehow she became tangled, and as she tried to unwind herself, the leash wrapped tighter and tighter around her body, pinning her against a tree trunk. I could see the leash cutting off her air supply and knew I needed to act fast. Delicate, utterly graceful Bandy transformed into a Tasmanian devil in a split second. She lashed out at everything to save herself, including my uncovered hands and arms as they reached up to help.

There was no time to prepare myself for the rescue with proper clothing and gloves. All I heard in my head was Sophie's voice telling me to protect Bandy at all costs. She tore at my flesh, blood spurting everywhere, but I was single-minded in my efforts to untangle her. Having heard the banshee screams, my housemates raced downstairs to see who was fighting, only to discover it was Bandy versus my limbs. Finally able to free her from the tree, I whisked her into the house, screaming for Sophie to remove her leash.

I slumped over the sink, my arms and hands shaking from the trauma, blood flowing freely into the sink. My housemates didn't realize how badly injured I was until they came over to the sink. Then they were horrified. But at least I got kudos from Sophie for keeping my promise.

That night, I shook with fever. I highly recommend that anyone in the position I was in seek medical care immediately, which I did not do. Bandy was also not happy. She spent the next few hours giving me the meanest stares, and over the next few days, wouldn't let me near her. By day three, we buried the hatchet. I held her and explained why I'd done what I'd done. Her eyes held mine as I spoke, and she seemed to soften.

The trauma of this episode stayed with Bandy longer than I would have imagined. She responded the same way the first time an outside cat took a swat at her. She looked hurt, emotionally distraught, studying the cat as if wondering why it would do that. Exactly as a child brought up in the safe and nurturing environment of a loving home might feel when pushed on the playground for the first time. Being treated like that is just not in their experience. They don't know meanness or violence. It makes no sense to them.

My encounter with Bandy certainly lingered with me for a long time, too. The problem with cat bites and scratches is that virulent infection is a real possibility. Especially with puncture wounds. When they happen, bacteria is deposited quickly and deeply into the host. Then, almost immediately, the wound closes up, trapping the bacteria inside. As my condition worsened, I looked online to determine what antibiotics were best for my type of injury. Self-administering antibiotics is frowned upon for good reason. But my experience in Nepal and India got me accustomed to the idea. Everything was self-administered there. Any drug you might want was available over the counter. Opiates for pain, Flagyl and Bactrim for parasites, steroids, ketamine, Valium, you name it. I was still of that mind-set.

Maybe it was the delirium of the fever that caused a familiar contemplation, but where does one draw the line when trying to implement nonviolence and compassion?

A central belief in Jainism, one of India's oldest religions, is ahimsa, or nonviolence. Some Jains will wear masks so as not to harm insects in the air they might otherwise breathe in, and will sweep the path in front of them before walking, to move away any creature they might otherwise harm. Sure, I care for the cats, but how many millions of living organisms do I kill every single day by driving my car, gargling with mouthwash, just walking down the sidewalk?

And how many more would be killed by the antibiotics I was about to take? I met a woman saint from India who wouldn't walk on the grass because of the pain she was aware she would be causing each blade. Where do you draw the line? Can I save cats and kill everything else in my unconscious, consumptive life and still have a clear conscience? Or do I have to be like the fourth-century monk Arya Asanga, who removed maggots from a dog's festering leg with his tongue because picking them out by hand was causing them too much pain? It is a dilemma we all come to terms with in our own way.

As luck would have it, I had in my closet a full dose of the very antibiotic recommended online; it had been prescribed to me for an ailment that remedied itself. I began taking the antibiotic and saw almost immediate improvement. The inflamed wounds on my arms and balloon-like hands began to reduce in intensity. Then one night I had a dream that gangrene had set in and doctors told me I would lose three fingers on my hand.

Enough with playing doctor. The next morning I hurried to the emergency room. The examining doctor told me he had hospitalized many people with much less severe injuries from cat bites, and had I seen him on the day of my injury, he would've admitted me on the spot. As it turned out, he told me I had taken the exact antibiotic in the exact dosage he would've prescribed for me, and felt confident self-administering that antibiotic is what saved my hand. He gave me an antibiotic boost by IV and sent me on my way with a fresh prescription (which I didn't take, in case another mauling was in my future!).

When I arrived home, there on the doormat, placed perfectly at its center, was a heavy work glove. A gift from Baby Gray. As if to say, "Use gloves next time, idiot."

After Pierre had come into her power — and she's certainly one of the largest and strongest of the colony — I had her outside on the leash one day, when Marble sauntered past. For some reason, Pierre puffed up her chest and decided to swat at her. Initially Marble cowered and began to sulk away, but then she thought about it a minute. Looking back at Pierre, perhaps realizing she was just a large baby, Marble turned and hit her back twice as hard, causing Pierre to run.

What amazes me to this day is that all three sisters have so much animosity toward Marble. They have no history with her whatsoever. In fact, they are related. Being Snow White's mother, Marble is their grandmother. Still, if the sisters are upstairs at night sitting on my windowsill, as they often are, one glimpse of Marble outside will send all three racing downstairs, hissing, throwing their bodies at the mesh door, trying to get at her. Even delicate Bandy.

And they're not the only ones. Gumdrop, the small, gentle calico that helps every cat in need, goes absolutely insane when she spots Marble. The first time I saw this happen, I had Gumdrop on a body leash. The moment she saw Marble in the bushes in the distance, she went after her with such force she snapped the leash and caught her in a matter of seconds, then a vicious fight ensued. Since then, I've always kept an extra firm grip on Gumdrop's leash when Marble is around. Still, Gumdrop will pant and growl and pant some more, tugging on the leash, whenever she catches sight of Marble. These two do have history, however. There was a time when Marble used to pick on Gumdrop. That all changed when Marble reappeared after being gone so long.

Finally, with respect to the Cutesies, my housemates and I are in agreement that they are the most sublime, integrated, exquisite cats we have ever known. It's hard to put into words, but anyone who has spent time with these sisters agrees they are like angels come to earth in the form of cats. To us, they feel like the souls of all the cats we have lost over the years coming back to us to bring us comfort and love. I couldn't think of a better last litter. An appropriate end to the lineage.

Charlie enjoying his throne.

15 Daily Grind

After six months of effort, all the cats were fixed, and with our feline family stabilized, we established a daily routine. Our day actually began with airing out our attached garage the night before, sometimes waiting until 4:00 AM before it was free of exhaust fumes. It was in the garage that the three sisters — Cozy, Pierre, and Bandy — slept every night, along with their "mother," Charlie, whom we brought in each night. It took at least two hours to air out the garage, depending on how far the cars had been driven, so if Heather or Sophie arrived home late at night, it could make for long nights of waiting. I'd become an expert at late-night jewelry shopping and could mimic info-mercials to the word.

The garage had four windows and a rear door. Onshore breezes were most welcome, since the cross ventilation moved fumes out more quickly. Once the exhaust had dissipated to our satisfaction, then car covers could be put in place. Atop Sophie's car roof, we sculpted a large green-felt tarp into an inviting cat bed, where the three sisters nestled themselves around Charlie, who lay in the middle. At times, the sisters would fall asleep sprawled over Charlie's body after he'd groomed each one diligently. This particular personality of his only came out at night. Should he see the sisters outside on their leashes during the day, when he ran with the colony, he'd hardly give them a second glance.

Tiny also slept in the garage. After several years of sleeping together on my bed, we came to a mutual decision that we both slept better with her in the garage. She curled up on a brown vel-veteen oval doughnut that complemented her coloring, placed on top of Heather's hood. And Gumdrop's white velveteen oval bed was situated on the dryer, which she vaulted onto with one leap before assuming her sleeping position. Since twice dislocating her elbow, she slept with her arm tucked under her chest and covered by her head, to protect the arm.

First thing in the morning, Gumdrop and Charlie were re-leased from the garage, fed, and let out for the day. They both spent their days unsupervised and without the restriction of har-nesses or leashes. Charlie was the more social of the two, cavort-ing with his colony family and friends, and entertaining neighbors who viewed him from afar. They recognized his vibrant spirit, even though he kept his distance. He was, after all, born of feral parents. Gumdrop, on the other hand, was a loner. She had no friends in the colony. So she spent her time alone, running in the overgrown fields of our neighbor's yard and finding solace in nature.

Now that Charlie and Gumdrop had begun their day, it was time to prepare breakfast for the outdoor colony, who now waited anxiously by the back door. Allies would rub against each other in anticipation of the meal, while enemies would hiss and growl, posturing for position. I liked to feed them smorgasbord style, though Sophie and Heather preferred to place small portions for each individual cat, paying special attention to Hyena, who ate away from the colony, under the lemon tree.

Once every cat had been fed and given fresh water, I swept the feeding area, and the colony retreated to the deep foliage out back, remaining hidden for much of the rest of the day. Tiny was let out whenever she wanted, since she always returned on her own.

Bandy, in her purple harness, began her day with a tour of the "jungle." First she crawled into the deep soil of her favorite plant, relishing its rich, loamy scent. Then she would be carried around to various trees, where she smelled their leaves before being lifted up high to swat at bugs she couldn't normally reach, even though she never snared them. Finally she roosted on her favorite sheltered tree stump, while her sister Cozy curled up in her birth nest, located just on the other side of the fence. And Pierre galloped atop the rotted fence, pretending she was unleashed and running wild across the veld in search of prey, a cat in the wild.

By the end of the day, all our leashed cats had been brought inside. The feral colony emerged from the dark folds of the underbrush and returned for dinner. After their feeding, I swept and then hosed down their concrete "dining table." After dark, I took the sisters back outside on their leashes to bask in the night air. There was more entertainment for them at this time, with the emergence of night insects. A praying mantis would keep them mesmerized for hours.

Late at night, if he wasn't already inside, which was rare, we would go in search of Charlie. If we didn't find him, he would cry outside Sophie's window in the early morning, making it impossible for her to sleep. He knew when we were searching for him and would roll in somersaults on the cement driveway in the distance, provoking us with playful cries. Then he would rub his body along the fence, pretending to look sleepy, and dart away just as we were ready to grab him. This game could last hours. Every. Single. Night.

Once the garage was aired out, I brought the sisters back inside and prepared everyone's bed. By this time, the cats couldn't wait to go into the garage, as if it were a slumber party with their best friends. And then the cycle repeated.

Princess walking along the fence.

16 Loss

Baby Gray's last litter before she was spayed consisted of four beautiful kittens, each of a different color. An orange tabby who became the famous Charlie, two torties, and a beautiful calico we had already named Patches. One day, for some reason, she placed them behind the air-conditioning unit against our back wall, where they lay exposed to predators. Prior to that, just as other mothers had, she kept them hidden behind the fence until it was time to show them off. But here they weren't safe. That night, as we tried to figure out a remedy for the situation, raccoons snatched Patches and one of the torties. Hearing their screams, I rushed out just as raccoons fled with both kittens. I couldn't save both, so I cornered the raccoon with the tortie in its mouth, screaming at it, pounding the fence. With nowhere to turn, it dropped the kitten and ran.

The little kitten stood against the fence, motionless. One remaining kitten, an orange tabby, remained in the nest unharmed. My housemates and I were mortified. These experiences were so gut wrenching it's hard to put into words. I approached the kitten against the fence, ready to bury yet another cat. The kitten appeared to have died standing up. As I got closer, however, I saw her breathing. Amazingly she was alive. I looked for blood around her and saw none. I took her carefully in my hands to see where the damage was, and I couldn't find any. And that's when I realized she was unscathed but frozen in stark terror.

There was no discussion about it. She and the orange tabby would be brought inside with us. We named them Princess and Charlie, and placed them in our closet in a large box filled with warm sheets and towels. Day after day, they did nothing but hug each other, staying absolutely silent, not a single cry.

Charlie endeared himself to every cat in the colony, females and males. That alone was quite the diplomatic feat. Princess, on the other hand, though loving, remained quite wild. Her teeth and nails cut like little razors. She spent most of her time outside and would sometimes be gone for days.

A favorite game of hers was to reenact her near-death experience. She would hide behind the fence on the jungle side and wait until everyone had arrived for mealtime. While the cats were busy eating, Princess, still invisible behind the fence, would make huge crashing sounds, hitting her body against the fence, breaking sticks and tearing leaves, growling deeply, causing everyone to run for their lives. Then, once the cats slowly returned to their food, she would come out of hiding and show everyone it was she who pretended to be a predator. She would strut back and forth as if to say she was so clever to have tricked them.

I don't know if it was for that reason or because she was so small, but every female cat in the colony had it in for her. Even the most docile were aggressive toward her. Making her way home was always an ordeal. She would wait until she spotted me and then hurry to me, using my legs as protection, and follow me into the house.

When I first found Princess as a kitten, Sophie said I called her the most beautiful cat I had ever seen. Maybe because of that or the abuse she suffered daily by other females, I gave her more attention than any other cat whenever I could. I fed her special meals, combed her, let her stay in my room.

A few short years later, the day Princess was killed, she had been sleeping all day inside. I decided she should go out rather than be restless inside all night. She was the one cat we never worried about outside; she was savvier than the entire rest of the colony put together. She never returned. The violent fracas we heard in the jungle that night must have indicated the time of her demise.

The next morning, a pall had fallen over the colony, and I knew something dreadful had happened. A massive windstorm started a few hours later and lasted for three days, knocking out power and leaving the entire neighborhood in darkness. Stores were quickly stripped clean of food and supplies. Trees and sign-posts were toppled; traffic was at a standstill. Sophie felt this freak storm to be Princess's fury — she wasn't ready to leave us.

Something died inside me the day Princess was killed. Years have passed since that tragic event, and time has healed no wounds. Her absence has left a void in my heart and a vacuum in the colony that can never be filled. The backyard jungle, the colony, the whole adventure would never be the same for me again. I searched my rolodex of teachings, sayings, aphorisms, life experiences, anything that would help, and came up empty. To come to terms with what life is — that everything cherished and loved will be lost, everyone held dear will be taken, sometimes in the most violent, seemingly ruthless manner — there really is no other response than crying until there are no more tears.

Nature had a lesson to share in Princess's passing, though. Her brother Charlie wasn't fazed in the least. Didn't miss a step. Though they had been extremely close, he didn't seem to give her a thought. Life went on; nothing existed for him but the present and what was about to happen in the next moment. It was something to behold, and a profound lesson.

Leo at rest.

17 Tiny and Leo's Ordeal

E very year, June becomes more meaningful, since it's the
month of both Father's Day and my mother's birthday.
With both my parents in their eighties, these times of celebration seem ever more poignant and significant to me. Enough
to make me drive across the Mojave Desert in 117-degree weather.
Testing fate with my rickety Nissan Altima, hoping it'll be good
for one more trip. And thankfully this year's trip was uneventful.
My parents know about the feral colony, and they ask about the
cats, but with an undertone of disappointment that it's not grandchildren they're asking about instead.

The night I arrived in Tucson, Sophie let me speak with all the indoor cats via Skype. She panned her computer across the room, zeroing in on each tucked in for the night. When she got to Tiny, she told me she was worried. She seemed sick, Sophie said, noting she was sitting in a place she hadn't before. I've learned to start paying attention when a cat sits somewhere unusual.

In this case, Tiny's signs were pronounced. I could see her ears folded down in front against her head. This was a sick cat indeed. Since Dr. V's passing, we had been unable to find a vet to replace him. The office had disbanded without any communication. And Stacey was nowhere to be found. Sophie said that every time I left home, some crisis hit the cats, and she was right. On top of that, Heather's cat, Leo, was suffering from feline immunodeficiency virus, which was incurable, and so his days were numbered.

I told Sophie she needed to move fast. She was running on just three hours of sleep a night due to overwhelming work at her office, so the last thing she needed was another responsibility. Especially one so close to the heart. But she and I agreed this was our baby, hand-raised from the start, and we would raise hell itself to help her.

First thing the next morning, she placed Tiny in her faux Louis Vuitton cat carrying case (nothing is too good for our girl) and took her to a nearby vet. Hearing that Tiny didn't struggle at all when placed into the cat carrier worried me all the more. The vet said Tiny had a fever of 106 that had probably been present for days, and she was worried about possible brain damage (a common theme, it seems, for our little cat). She wanted to watch Tiny walk to make sure no damage had already occurred.

After running tests, the vet told Sophie that Tiny was too sick for their facility and would need to be taken to an animal emergency hospital miles away.

Tiny was admitted and kept overnight, but didn't improve.

Hooked up to IVs for fluids and antibiotics, she still wasn't eating and wouldn't keep down what they force-fed her. There is a procedure whereby the food is placed directly into the stomach of the cat, but she was too weak. The vets felt she wouldn't survive the procedure.

After another day at the hospital, the vet strongly suggested Sophie take Tiny to a specialist who could help identify the cause of her illness. Sophie rushed her to the specialist that Friday, the last appointment they had before closing for the weekend. But the specialist was at a loss. She said tests could run as high as ten thousand dollars and still be inconclusive. Thankfully Sophie left that place in a hurry and returned to the animal hospital, where they welcomed Tiny back and returned her to IVs.

By this time, I was wearing away the carpet of my friend's Tucson townhouse, pacing back and forth as I spoke with Tiny's doctors. I explained to them that our feral tabby had once had a fever of 108 for five days until Dr. V came up with the right antibiotic mixture. One of the vets sounded encouraged to hear that and agreed to change Tiny's antibiotic cocktail every thirty-six hours if she wasn't responding to the current one.

The problem with a cat not eating is that in a short time the cat's liver begins to feed on itself. And once this happens, irreparable damage occurs.

Tiny's liver enzyme levels were very high, worrying us all that her liver was failing.

I went to dinner that evening wiping my constant tears, using the excuse of the salsa being too hot. I couldn't stop Tiny's life from flashing before my eyes. All her little gestures, her moods, her personality, our love for each other. I couldn't sleep that night. The summer nights in Tucson last a lifetime. Luckily the animal hospital was open twenty-four hours, so at daybreak I called to check on Tiny. No change, fever still high.

A few hours later, the vet called saying the steroid shots they had given Tiny reduced her fever but she still wouldn't eat. Later that day on the phone, Sophie and I commiserated with each other, and she said something that struck a nerve.

"It's up to us to save her."

I realized she was right. Again. I got on the phone and called several remote healers who got to work on her. I made offerings to priests, nuns, monks, and shamans to pray for her. Still it didn't seem enough.

I stood outside later that stark afternoon, the heat like an oven, the air still, looking up at the merciless clear sky. And there was Tiny, her presence so distinct. In my heart. Calling for me. That was all I needed. I ran back inside, packed all my things, gassed up the car, and drove back across the Mojave to be with her. By the way, the town of Quartzsite, at the border of Arizona and California, on a late Saturday night in summer, is one surreal scene. Situated in the middle of the desert. The only civilization for miles around. Parking lots teem with teenage goth ravers, survivalists living off the grid, wary middle-aged couples just stopping for gas, and hundreds of retirees who spend the year living in their recreational vehicles on Bureau of Land Management property strewn for miles on either side of Interstate 10.

The vets had left standing orders that I was to be allowed to see Tiny any time of the day or night and stay with her as long as I wanted. Talk about a great facility! Arriving in Los Angeles at 2:00 AM, I rushed to the hospital a half hour later, and the vet on call brought Tiny, with her still-attached IV, into a waiting room. She was seated like a loaf of bread. She didn't recognize me. She didn't recognize anything. I held her, wrapping my arms around her unmoving body. I realized that perhaps more than anything, I'd just wanted to see her one last time. Just to feel her fur and look into her eyes and tell her how much I loved her and that nothing would be the same if she left us. At 4:00 AM, the orderly came to check on me. Seeing me still embracing Tiny, he left.

The next day, the vet told me it was time to consider putting Tiny down. Nothing was making any difference, and she was suffering. I broke the news to Sophie, who could barely speak. I began calling cremation services for pets, but every time the person on the other end answered, I started sobbing so hard I couldn't speak and had to hang up. I fell face-first on my still-packed luggage, in gut-wrenching sobs, so long and hard my head pounded.

Across the hall, I heard Heather in her room crying, too, and found out she had been arranging for someone to come to the house to euthanize Leo. Heather cared for this cat like none other. She would cut evenings short and wake up early just to feed him on time. She would warm his food and carefully serve it, no matter how little she slept or busy she was. She would hand-make kitty litter rather than risk using toxic brands. And she worked ten years longer at her job than originally planned, just to pay off his expensive treatments when he was sick.

How in the world could this be possible, I wondered, that our two most precious cats would die on the same day? Realizing Leo was now the priority, I rushed to the store and purchased two dozen assorted-color roses and a card for him. I clipped the rose heads so they would surround his body, adding much-needed color and fragrance to the sad room. He kept looking at the roses as each was placed near him, and then I placed the card by his head. His kidneys had failed, so he was unable to move but was lying comfortably on a plush new white blanket. We all said our good-byes to Leo. It was as much to honor him as Heather, who had cared for him so diligently.

That afternoon, during the euthanasia, the wind blew softly, rattling our blinds, and the sun's rays turned golden, a hue I don't remember ever seeing. The light continued becoming more and more brilliant, as if the gates of heaven themselves had opened to let him in.

With Leo's passing, I had a sudden realization. It was as if he were telling me exactly what to do for Tiny. First he reminded me that, even on her best days, no way in hell was Tiny going to eat any other food but what we feed her. *Picky eater* doesn't even half describe her. Then he told me she needed familiar surroundings; she was scared and in shock. Of course.

I ran downstairs and washed out her food bowl, then grabbed the only food she'd eat and hurried to the hospital. When I arrived, I asked the orderly for a room far from the others. They brought Tiny in with attached IV. When she saw me she meowed in recognition, unkempt, but alert for the first time. Or was this the last? Was she just saying good-bye to me?

She watched as I spread out her familiar towel. Then she saw me fill her very own bowl with her favorite food and place it on the towel. I positioned her on my stomach and held her weak body against mine, her head flat against my chest. I began speaking quietly to her so she would hear my voice. After several hours, I thought I felt a purr. I kept at it, and yes, another purr. I kept this up all night. In the morning, the staff found me still with her.

The vet came into the room and told me that it really was time to put Tiny down. I started to cry, and my heaving chest bothered Tiny, so I moved her to the table. Wiping away the endless tears while the vet stood patiently by.

I soon realized the doctor wasn't so much looking at me as he was at Tiny. She had staggered over to her food bowl and, with emaciated mouth, tried to take a morsel of food. After working at it a while, she finally was able to get a single kernel of food past her dry lips, and crunched.

"No...way," the vet gasped.

This was the turning point. I spent the next two days with her around the clock, holding her against my chest the entire time, singing the songs we had composed and used to sing her. Soon she was purring nonstop, hour after hour, her head rubbing against my chin's stubble as she used to do as a kitten, burying her head into my armpit, letting me smooth out her matted hair and clean her eyes.

On the day she was released, everyone came to see her off. One veterinary assistant who hurried from the back to say good-bye to her looked familiar. I suddenly realized this was Stacey from Dr. V's office, whom we had looked so hard to find. Seeing her, I burst into tears. She explained that she had been under a noncompetition agreement and so couldn't advertise her whereabouts.

We now don't take good health for granted. Things can change so quickly and dramatically with animals. Tiny came home and returned to her routines, but she had changed. The trauma of her illness and being in the hospital had impacted her. She didn't have the strength to jump, though she tried. She also developed some different meows while in the hospital, and she looks more feminine now for some reason, with newly formed dark lines around her eyes that make her look like she's wearing mascara. As much as we loved her before, we relish every moment with her now.

Ironically, soon thereafter, I began to feel ill. As my body continued to weaken, I became quite certain something was seriously wrong. Then I started to lose muscle tone and mass, and began having delirious dreams, waking up in the morning certain that I had died overnight. I spent much of the day in a ball on the ground curled up with my head on the floor, shaking with rigors, breathing in cat hair and who knows what else.

It was all I could do to just keep breathing and hope that my system wouldn't shut down completely. For the first time in my life, I realized it was possible I might not recover from an illness. As bad as flu bugs can be, you can always ride them out. But this felt different.

Sophie helped where she could, loading me up with supplements and powdered proteins to help bolster my constitution. Until finally I asked her to drop me off at the emergency room of a nearby hospital. Many people had recently joined Obamacare, and the hospital had recently implemented a new computer system, so it was nine hours before I was seen.

Despite the wait, and as much as I loathe emergency rooms, I was elated to be there, just hoping the doctors would be able to get to the bottom of things. Many hours and tests later, nothing turned up positive, and I was released. I knew if they sent me home, I would get worse, but the doctors told me they had no reason to keep me.

Things did get worse. And once again, I asked to be taken to the emergency room. Another daylong wait followed by more negative tests. Released again, and back to the emergency room again a few days later.

This time, I exhibited symptoms that concerned the doctors enough to admit me to the hospital. For days, I underwent a barrage of tests, a million-dollar workup. Exasperated when everything came back negative, the doctors were open to suggestions. So I had them check me for HIV, Lyme disease, even toxoplasmosis, a parasite that can be contracted from cats. Nothing.

Being away from the house and cat responsibilities was surprisingly restful. Even being awakened every two hours in the hospital by nurses taking blood or giving me medicine was like staying at a resort compared to how I had been living. I hadn't realized the cumulative level of stress I had been under all those years.

In the past, when I left town, I would initially receive emails and texts from my housemates sharing vignettes about the cats and reports on how everyone was doing. Then, after a few more days, I'd receive messages sent by "the cats," saying that Mommy (Sophie) wasn't cutting it and I needed to come home immediately because things were going to hell. And if I stayed away any longer, I'd receive messages too vulgar to reveal.

But when I was in the hospital, all of that changed. My housemates would've cared for the cats for months if needed, without a resentful word, so they said.

Doctors were never able to determine the cause of my illness, though there was some speculation it was neurologically based. Even today I'm somewhat compromised. The only anomaly that stood out for the specialists was my caring for the cats. And though no doctor spoke it aloud, I could see their brains spinning, thinking that somehow the cats were the culprits.

When I finally returned home, the cats I'd thought I might never meet again looked marvelous, as if I were seeing them for the first time. Their colors and personalities so vivid and bright.

When Tiny looked up at me, I realized she had some sense of my ordeal. From that moment on, she wouldn't leave my side. Just as I had held her newly sutured stomach for weeks after her surgery, she kept her body pressed solidly against mine at all times. She never left my bed, always with a part of her body draped over mine, or lying on top of me. If I would move, she moved in step. Even today, a year later, Tiny rarely leaves my side. Sophie remarks that as bonded as we were before, now it's like we've become one. Is this a sign of reciprocity?

Tiny grew to be not so tiny.

18 Moving

A Buddhist teacher from Asia visited California some years back. His students spared no expense in making sure he was well cared for, including securing a scenic home for him situated high on the cliffs overlooking the Pacific Ocean. When the teacher arrived, he surveyed the beautiful setting and, after acknowledging the efforts made by his students, gently asked to be moved away from the ocean. He found the suffering of the sea creatures almost unbearable.

I guess it boils down to perception. Perception for most of us is subjective, and limited. Even the mechanics of perception. Our visual range itself covers but a small part of the entire electromagnetic spectrum. Even things we do see aren't as they appear. An apple looks red, when in fact the apple is every color but red. That's because every color is absorbed by the object except for the one we see, which is reflected off the object and is not the object's true color at all.

This question of perception became a daily contemplation for me with respect to the cats. Am I correctly perceiving what the cats are needing or not needing at any given time? And on a greater scale, I contemplated nature itself. Could my personal needs and desires — even the desire to help — relax? Could I trust in the rhythm and intelligence of nature so that I could be a perfect tool of support rather than one of obstruction, on even the most minute level?

If I could misinterpret the color of an apple, what else was I missing?

I heard a teacher in Nepal once tell a story about various types of beings standing at a riverbank watching the water flow by. Those from the demonic realms perceived the water as fire. Hungry ghosts saw water as pus and blood. Fish recognized the water as home. Humans perceived it simply as life-supporting water. And gods perceived water as nectar.

I could relate to this story by recalling challenges in my life that I initially perceived as horrible — similar to mistaking water for fire — but that, in the long run, were actually beneficial. And I could see how, for instance, a person — or a feral cat — running scared might misinterpret a helping hand for poison and turn away from it. Perception.

One thing I knew for sure: amid the myriad philosophical and practical possibilities my housemates and I struggled with every day, one constant was the bedrock of our home. Cats need stability, protection, and routine. They need a home. And so did we. We were a family. We often reflected on how lucky we were to have found a place of safety for us all in such a large urban setting.

But that all unexpectedly changed one night when our landlord ran alongside the door of Sophie's car as she pulled into the driveway. The landlord had a concerned look on her face. Her brother, it seemed, had decided to move to the States from Hong Kong and would need to move into our house. The house actually belonged to him. While we'd always known that he could ask for it back at any time, after twenty years, we assumed we were safe. But we were wrong.

And we were devastated. Once again, perception had failed us. We'd mistaken our house of cards for a solid base. That's what death is — from the small deaths that occur every moment in life, the millions of cells that die every second, to the final parting, everything and everyone in one's life are eventually taken. And this was a reminder. The news cut to the bone and put us in shock. Our initial reaction of wondering how we would land on our two feet quickly changed to wondering how our cats were going to land on four!

Our landlord, who lived in the house in front of ours, had no idea of the extent of our cat caregiving. She suspected things at times, from the stain of fish oils from the food seeping into the concrete slab of our backyard or my creeping around her house at all hours like a thief whenever one of our cats would get loose. For some reason, our escaped cats loved hiding near the landlord's house. I quickly ran out of excuses when, after hearing all the noise I was making searching under woodpiles and metal cans, her husband came running from the house looking for prowlers. When our landlord occasionally wondered out loud why cats prowled the area, I'd mention I saw the old ladies next door tossing them food, and the topic would be forgotten for a few months.

The news of our having to move seemed to disturb the landlord nearly as much as us. She'd been able to keep the rent low all these years by convincing her brother that the sisters were like family. And they were, having watched the landlord's daughters grow from toddlers into the mature women they became.

Our egos convince us we will live forever. People who know exactly how long they have to live are said to be fortunate, as life's priorities shift and become very clear. Now that our time had come, our perception of the neighborhood did in fact change. The constant noise, the cigarette and marijuana smoke wafting from the neighbors' yards, the ubiquitous sickening smell of scented dryer sheets we lived downwind of, courtesy of a neighbor running an illegal laundry service. The gang in the house kitty-corner across the street, with their rotation of family members going in and coming out of prison, and something of a makeshift halfway house in their backyard, with ex-cons sleeping in the grass and fighting most nights. The huge German shepherds kept by the neighbors next to them that barked day and night ten feet from my bedroom window, in a yard of concrete that amplified the sound, making it seem they were using megaphones. Even today, I still wake up every five minutes in a sweat, my system so used to being jolted from sleep. All these things seemed precious now.

In retrospect, losing our house shouldn't have come as a total surprise. Days before we received the news, for the first time in her life, Gumdrop had run from the house and didn't return for three days. On the day of her return, we received the news about having to move. There are numerous accounts of animals heading en masse for higher ground prior to the Indian Ocean tsunami of 2004. They just know.

Our reminiscing and getting nostalgic didn't keep our stomachs from churning, however. This was a disaster. One of the worst things for cats is change. We had spent years trying to create stability, to help bring normalcy to cats who before had only known chaos.

The sisters and I sat in the living room, stunned. One thing we knew for certain was that the outside colony could not be moved. This decision was confirmed by conversations I had on the phone in the next few frantic hours with our vet and feral-cat-rescue organizations. Unless we could find an expanse of property, like a ranch or a large barn, somewhere safe from predators, with caretakers to feed and care for them, the colony would need to remain here.

Considering what to do with the cats we kept inside was almost as daunting. These were not lap cats. They didn't cuddle. They did not wear collars; nor were they immunized or microchipped. They were born of the wild and would remain wild, which was just as we felt it should be.

For days, I felt frozen. A pall fell over the house, making it seem like a mausoleum. Sounds had no resonance. A vacuum. There was no solution, and we knew it. The sisters and I would pass each other in the hallway like zombies, afraid to make eye contact lest the recognition of how screwed we were should inadvertently be shared with a glance.

Since I wasn't eating, drinking, or sleeping, I had lots of time to turn over our dilemma in my mind, until finally, in a burst of blasphemy, I looked to the heavens and screamed, "This one's on you! You've just sentenced these cats to death. The blood's on your hands, not mine! This is all on you!"

Startled at my outburst, I sat contritely, waiting for a lightning bolt to come crashing through the roof with my name on it.

Instead, Sophie yelled upstairs that we were out of cat food. Going to PetSmart for kibbles for their "last meal" was not top on my list. But I figured it was better than guaranteeing my seat in hell by cursing the heavens. I drove to the store with a heavy heart. I realized once again it all came down to money. Not having financial resources, I couldn't care for the cats the way they needed to be cared for. The obvious choice would be to buy a ranch and move all the cats there. So I meekly recanted my rant at heaven and instead berated myself. The blood was on my hands, I realized. I couldn't provide for my family.

At the pet store, I loaded up the cart for the last time, then made my way to the cat-adoption cages, a routine I've maintained for years. I greet each cat, tell them how lovely they are and how certain I am that a loving family will be adopting them soon. I once fell in love with one of those caged cats and would visit her often. One day, I happened to casually mention my infatuation with this cat to the sisters, and they shook me by the shoulders, yelling, "Have you lost your mind?! Bring another cat into this house?!"

This time, I found the cages empty. The cats had been moved to the front of the store to show them off for adoption, an effort run by a jovial middle-aged woman named Jasmine and her volunteers. Things were frantic around the cages as closing time neared, giving children but a few precious final minutes to convince their parents they couldn't live without the cat they had already fallen in love with. Jasmine looked like she had been through this many times before, as she answered questions, no matter how trivial, with patience and ease. "No, the ear hasn't been damaged. That is a universal sign the cat has been fixed."

Turning to me with the smile of a nun, she asked, "Are you looking to adopt a cat?"

"No," I whispered back. "I'm looking to find a home for a bunch of semiferal cats we raised. And a colony of fully feral cats that still live outside."

I briefly described our dilemma, while she glanced left and right. She then signaled, with a tilt of her head, to follow her to the corner of the room. Mother Teresa morphed into James Bond. She was part of a large network of people who can help in these situations, she whispered. This was the feral-cat underground, the deep web of felines, covert ops. She needed no further explanation; I was one of them.

She knew firsthand the necessity of secrecy. She lived in a rented apartment where she was allowed two cats. She had twenty-five. Her main complaint: "Why can't they vacuum while I'm away?"

I said, "Yeah, and cook."

She gave me back a steely-eyed glare. "No, just vacuum."

She explained that it hadn't started out that way, that she'd been perfectly content with her two cats. But when discarded cats were left in bags at the doors of pet stores and vets after hours, she would inevitably get the call. Her first impulse, she explained, was always "No, I can't take in another cat." Her second impulse was always "Why not?" The routine was always the same. Once a new cat was introduced to her brood, her alpha males and females would sniff them all around and then return to their thrones with a nod of approval. Everyone was always accepted.

She said it was black cats that were abandoned most often. Superstitions carried over from medieval Europe, no doubt. I knew what she meant.

In considering our options for the indoor cats, I contacted a cat sanctuary. There they would be fed and kept safe. Perhaps. But unlike the domestic cats that made up their population, ours were semiferal, and never the twain shall meet. Like slipping Africanized bees into a honeybee colony.

I began to be influenced by a friend who, on hearing of our dilemma, said, "Andrew, this is your opportunity to free yourself of this burden. These cats are like a weight around your neck. You can't go anywhere, and you're spending money you don't have. They'll take the love you raised them with and move on to the next chapter of their lives." I countered that this was my family and that I had committed myself to them for life when I first got involved. But he took that as a nice story that had grown stale and guessed that, deep down, even I didn't believe it anymore. Maybe he was right.

Once again at a crossroads and not clear about a true direction, I still refused to believe feral cats were dispensable.

"Mother Nature doesn't make mistakes," explained Melya Kaplan in an article about her innovative Working Cats Program in Los Angeles. "We probably just haven't found a purpose for them yet."

Working Cats is an arm of the Voice for the Animals Foundation, a nonprofit animal advocacy and rescue group. Feral cats with no hope for adoption and slated to join the millions killed each year at animal shelters, have been enlisted to control rodents at private and commercial properties, even schools.

To date, the organization has placed about five hundred cats in nearly fifty locations, including the Los Angeles Police Department. When introduced to a new location, the cats are put in large wire holding cages and housed in a shed for a month to help them acclimate to their new environment.

"You can't just take feral cats and put them in one location and expect them to stay," Kaplan said. "A feral cat will kill himself trying to get back to his old location."

It takes about thirty days for a feral cat to become comfortable enough to consider a new location its home turf.

One example is the Original Los Angeles Flower Market. Impervious to normal methods of extermination, vermin at the flower market scared customers, nibbled on flowers, and even chewed through the wooden refrigerator where flowers were stored. Now cats named Pacino and DeNiro are wardens at the Original Los Angeles Flower Market.

The success of the Working Cats Program, says Kaplan, is thanks to the fact that adding a predator to the environment will scare away its prey. It's not so much that cats kill rodents; it's that rodents smell the cats' scent and decide to go elsewhere.

But the feral cat needs to stay feral. If a cat suddenly gets friendly, the animal is pulled from the program and, with any luck, adopted.

I wished I had heard of Working Cats sooner, but now I was running out of time. My best alternative seemed to be pursuing the cat sanctuary option. I found a facility near Fresno that could take all the cats, but they charged five thousand dollars per cat to care for them for life. There was another in South Bay, Los Angeles, but they only accepted terminally ill cats. There were a few local sanctuaries, but they either didn't have room or received horrible reviews. That left me with one choice, a place near Santa Monica, which I decided to visit in person.

Dozens of cats had the run of the open-air rooms. I waded through piles of cats as I explored each room, trying to imagine my cats being there. The caretaker of the place told me theirs was a nonprofit organization and that cats were kept there for life unless they were adopted. I asked if I could reclaim my cat after leaving it there a month or two, and he said I could pay a little more to keep it from being adopted, but I would not be able to reclaim the cat myself — a friend would need to do it on my behalf. He had no answer as to why.

Then he asked how old my cats were.

I said, "Well, one was born in 2010, and..."

"That one will cost two thousand dollars," he said in all seriousness.

"Really, that much?"

"It's all based on age."

I decided to lie about my next cat. "Another was born in 2013."

"Eight hundred dollars."

I could see where this was headed fast. But in fairness, I know how much vet bills can run, and if you're caring for cats for life, no doubt you need a war chest.

Still, I had to ask, "You sure you guys are nonprofit?"

He nodded, still serious, then added, "And there's a surcharge for black cats — two thousand five hundred dollars each."

Somehow I couldn't hear that any other way but racist.

"Nobody wants to adopt a black cat," he rationalized.

"That's just pure black cats, right?"

"No. Even a black freckle on an otherwise nonblack cat. Two thousand five hundred dollars."

"You're kidding me."

His look told me he wasn't.

I pulled out my phone and perused images of our cats, and lo and behold, they all had black on them somewhere. Even orange tabby Charlie had a small black mark on his side. I showed him the image, and he gave me the twenty-five-hundred-dollar nod. For a spot the size of a mole. That was the end of that idea.

I began looking for long-term pet hotels and the like, because it seemed impossible we would find another place to live so quickly and even less likely they would allow pets, let alone six cats.

I began contacting everyone I knew, regardless of where they lived. Did they know of a protected expanse of property, a secure barn, anything that could house our indoor cats, and even better if we could move the entire outside colony there as well? Nothing panned out. The underground railroad of feral-cat placement dried up, too, despite how promising it initially seemed. I was put into contact with people by text, and queries went out; but either everyone's house was already full, or newly established properties weren't ready to accept cats yet. Had I found a home for them, I'm not even sure how well they would've survived. They had bonded so strongly with us. And I felt even more certain about it when recalling a line from *The Little Prince*: "You become responsible, forever, for what you have tamed."

A very wise friend then sent me a message saying, "They are your responsibility. Take care of your cats." That certainly resonated with me, but I guess I needed more convincing, because I noticed on the car in front of me the bumper sticker "Don't Abandon Your Baby." I thought, Really? I don't mind hints from the universe, but isn't this overkill?

That left me but one option. There was a townhouse in Tucson, Arizona, I could rent, and possibly buy. According to the home owners' association, there was no restriction on cats. This was a viable option. The move would be difficult on the cats, just as it would be difficult for me. Caring for all the cats by myself in a one-thousand-square-foot place where everything from cacti to scorpions, bobcats, wild boar, and rattlers would be foreign to them, as would be the torturous heat.

Every time Sophie thought of never seeing the cats or me again, she would burst into tears. And my dilemma was, every time I flew to Tucson to visit the townhouse, I found myself peering out from my window seat praying that the plane would go down. I hated being in Tucson that much. So obviously we needed other options.

Heather would move in with her mother, and that left no room for Sophie. She rationalized, correctly, that two people can rent much more house than one person alone, and so we went to work searching. Our days were spent with her on the computer and me driving countless miles viewing the houses she found, from Altadena to Glendale, Eagle Rock, San Gabriel, and Arcadia, every neighborhood in the San Gabriel Valley. Each place I saw was problematic for one reason or another. Either massive power lines through the backyard, sketchy neighborhoods, or gorgeous places in the pictures turning out to be pigsties in person. All required one-year leases, while we barely had enough money for a deposit. Most wouldn't allow pets, and I didn't blame them. I wouldn't want a few cats living in my rental, let alone a half dozen.

And the problem was, by the following Monday, I would have to leave for Tucson if I was going to take the townhouse, making Sunday our line in the sand. After getting quotes from professional cat movers, and even checking the FAA regulations on transporting cats by plane, I decided to rent an SUV large enough to carry all the cats and purchased a pet carrier for each of them. When I got the official quote back from the car rental agency, they had forgotten to add the drop-off fee since I was just driving the vehicle one way. I took that as a sign that I was Tucson bound.

It wasn't even a matter of whether we could afford a place or not; we'd be living off borrowed funds regardless. This was a decision being made for the cats. As one house after another got crossed off the list, I began to give up hope. And I was tired of looking. My last stop was a place in Arcadia. I had been in La Cañada looking at a home and, as I jumped on the freeway for Arcadia, noticed the exit for Mount Wilson. I had always wanted to visit the six-thousand-foot peak, but now I just wanted to gain perspective, to drop my problems in the valley below and get some altitude.

I drove the winding roads, feeling lighter and lighter as I ascended. I ventured only about halfway up the mountain and then pulled off at a vista point. I breathed deep of the mountain air and prayed for clarity. Being in nature soothed my soul, and when I realized the afternoon was slipping away and I still needed to see the Arcadia house, I reluctantly returned to the salt mines.

The deep golden glow of the setting sun accented the large house when I pulled up. In the front yard, I saw three peacocks fully unfurled strutting just for me. A spark lit up inside. That meant something. I knew that meant something. I just sat in the car, watching, when a peahen came alongside my car. Peering from the window, I saw that at her feet were three chicks she was proudly displaying. These were signs!

I walked the property and peered through the windows. The house looked somewhat run down, but the property was beautiful, with persimmon and hibiscus trees in full bloom, along with a large juniper tree, jasmine bushes, and Japanese maples. I could imagine our cats frolicking among all the foliage. I called the broker and asked if he could show me the house immediately. He said he could do it on Thursday.

Thursday took an eternity to arrive. Once inside, Sophie and I saw that the house was indeed tired, with stained wooden floors and sad rooms. But it was large and surrounded by million-dollar homes and was library quiet. Anyway, I wanted a tired house. That way any damage the cats might cause wouldn't even be noticed. The owner just needed someone to rent the place for six months before he remodeled it anyway. It was the only short-term rental we had found.

Sophie wasn't so sure. I told her to just look at it as a staging area. A place where we could catch our breath. And besides, we hadn't found anything else. Basically, either it was this place or I was headed to Tucson. She finally agreed. This began a whirlwind of paperwork and rental contracts.

Meanwhile we needed to pack up decades of living and hired a team to scour the place of twenty years of dirt and grime. Boxes filled the house; the garage had piles that needed to be gone through. The outside colony most certainly smelled change in the air and came as a group each night to sit with us. They wouldn't move from the back porch. I spoke to each one over and over again, explaining that this hadn't been our plan, that we'd never meant to leave them. And I reminded them how strong and independent they had been before we arrived and said they would need to be that way again. For all I know, I was just talking to myself. But they sat and listened to my voice intently, once again in a semicircle. It felt like closure. Like I had fulfilled my commitment to them.

Beige was particularly somber. He curled up as he never had before, a look in his eyes unlike any I had seen, save for a friend of mine who knew she was dying but never told anyone. It was a look I'll never forget. I spoke to the indoor cats, too, while they slept. Like being on the verge of divorce and peeking into your sleeping children's rooms for the last time, knowing that their world would soon never be the same. And they had no clue.

I had some concern about moving Charlie, in that he was the alpha male and spent most of his time outdoors. When he's indoors too long, his constant foghorn of a cry can drive us mad. I also cringed at the idea of removing him from the colony. His mother, Baby Gray; his love, Snow White; and the rest of the cats would miss him terribly. On the other hand, the thought of not moving him with the three sisters — Bandy, Pierre, and Cozy, who had bonded with him as with a mother — was equally sad.

The cat I was most concerned about moving with, however, was Pierre. A refined and powerful yet extremely delicate cat, she's like a Ferrari. She takes a lot of work and constant maintenance, but when she's running well, she's exquisite. Yet the smallest issue can put her up on blocks and set her back months.

Despite the pep talk I'd given the colony, I still had concern for them. I considered their dilemma from every angle, until some ancient memory percolated to the surface. It was a lingering question I had had since first encountering the colony twenty years earlier: Who had been caring for these cats before we arrived? Because things were in full swing by the time we got there, and the cats seemed relatively healthy.

I thought back to the time I'd spotted someone throw a slab of meat onto the lid of their garbage cans, obviously with the cats in mind. Through the slats of our shared fence, I'd seen a wisp of white hair, a stooped woman in a housecoat, and for years later I'd wondered about it.

There was a duplex to our south, and I was betting the white-haired woman lived in one of the two units. Both occupants were recluses, rarely venturing out. Their stucco homes were shrouded in heavy yet neat undergrowth accented by palm trees, and they kept macaws in cages hanging on their verandas. Behind the duplex was another home partitioned into single rooms that were rented out to all kinds of unsavory-looking individuals, making it a familiar stop for police officers and a breeding ground for what I'd discovered one night, when I was bored and searched online, was a bevy of sex offenders. Is *bevy* the right word? A *posse* of sex offenders? A *gaggle*?

I discovered that the duplex was home to three elderly Hispanic women. The woman occupying the half of the duplex closer to us was frumpy and slow moving, with a mop of white hair. She must've been the one I saw through the slatted fence years before. The other half of the duplex housed an elegant woman with the chiseled features and demeanor of a person who was wise to the world. She lived with her mother, who was ancient yet able to get around with help from her daughter. The residents of the two units were friends, as it turned out. The other thing they shared, which I found out when knocking on their doors to discuss the cat situation, was the inability to speak a word of English — or so they said.

Still, I felt in my gut these women were our cat saviors.

And I had an easy remedy for the language barrier: Sophie. Not only fluent in Spanish, she'd been a Spanish major. The key would be to have discussions with these neighbors stealthily, without our landlord seeing. Sophie and I hurried out the front door and nonchalantly passed in front of our landlord's house so as not to provoke suspicion. The elegant woman saw us walking up her driveway and was neutral, neither welcoming of us nor resistant.

Sophie began speaking and the woman remained nonreactive. It took a few minutes for Sophie's Spanish to kick in, but once it did, the first reaction from the woman (which is always the case, every time I've seen Sophie speak Spanish with a native speaker) was awe. It was one thing to hear fluent Spanish coming from the mouth of a nonnative speaker, still another to hear the refined quality of her Spanish. Formal, just like it's spoken in Spain. I've seen even the most stoic people crack — that curl of the lips, the shaking head, and the familiar question, "How the hell did you learn to speak Spanish like that?"

Which is exactly what this woman asked, after introducing herself as Ana. As the conversation wore on, I could see that though Ana had warmed to Sophie as a person, she was not keen about what she was hearing.

Then it struck me. "Tell her these aren't our cats. We're not asking her to care for our cats. These are cats in the wild. They were here when we first moved in." When Sophie told her, Ana's eyes lit up. Sophie translated the rest of their exchange for me:

Yes, Ana explained, she had seen them. "A white one with blue eyes."

"Yes!" Sophie said.

"A few gray ones." Then Ana beamed. "And that yellow one!"

Of course, Charlie.

Yes, we nodded with smiles. She agreed to put out water for them, and food when she could.

"Is there a particular type of food they like?" she wondered.

That was my cue. I sauntered back to the house, passing the landlord's home as if going for a stroll. Once out of sight, I sprinted into our house, grabbed a bag of cat food, and hiding it under my arm, meandered back to Ana's home. Sophie explained to her we were willing to pay any and all expenses, including vet bills should a cat get sick. She refused any help with expenses but mentioned that the woman who lived in the duplex next door could use the money. And Ana added that the woman liked cats. She was in Mexico at that time but was to return in a matter of days.

So concerned was I about the well-being of the outside cats

that I held a vigil outside of that woman's house, counting the hours before she would arrive home from Mexico. Carrying moving boxes out of the house one day, I finally spotted the white-haired lady trimming bushes in her dense garden out front. We waved to each other as I approached, and we spoke across the hedge in hushed tones, even though our landlord didn't understand Spanish.

I began to tell her about our move, but she just smiled, shook her head, and with an apologetic shrug said that she didn't speak English. I tried again, saying we had lived there "veinte años." She gestured to her house with a smile and said, "Cuarenta años." Aha, I thought, forty years. Maybe she *had* been the colony's caregiver before we arrived. Gesturing with my hands and wracking my brain to recall anything from elementary school Spanish class.

"No...vaya, por favor."

"No te vayas," she said, correcting my broken Spanish. "Sí, sí, okay," she agreed.

Not caring if the landlord saw me racing across her lawn, I burst through the door yelling to Sophie that the white-haired lady was waiting to speak to her. Sophie hurried down the stairs, and we both sauntered out of the house as if going for a walk — looking up at the trees, admiring the neighbor's lawn — until we reached the patiently waiting older woman. She welcomed us.

Sophie began speaking in Spanish, and that familiar smile spread across the woman's face. But instead of complimenting Sophie on the quality of her language skills, she began telling her what a shame it was that they had never become friends, since we had been neighbors for so long. Her husband had died, and she had been so lonely. She so wished she had had someone to talk to in Spanish all these years.

It was a poignant moment, perhaps repeated in many neighborhoods. People being so caught up in life that they forget the human element, the rich interactions waiting and available just next door. It also struck me as remarkable that a bunch of cats had made this moment happen. Were it not for the cats, we would have left the neighborhood never realizing how much we truly were leaving behind.

She introduced herself as Camila and began to tell us how, many years before, she had begun caring for wild cats that lived deep in the underbrush our houses shared. Her love of cats began then, she explained. Then neighbors in the apartment complex next door abandoned five cats when they moved, which she took in and cared for. Of the five, one she was most enamored with before he died was just like an orange tabby she often saw running around here, she explained.

Charlie, of course. Everyone loves Charlie! Sophie shared with her the name we had given him, and she giggled. She remarked how much she missed her orange tabby.

Sophie described our dilemma to her, and she nodded in understanding. She felt confident she could leave food out for them very close to where we had been feeding them all those years, and water, too. As with Ana, we offered to pay for any and all expenses. She didn't have a car or a way to get around, so we told her we would provide all the food she needed. We shared phone numbers and promised to stay in touch.

It was now Saturday, and the car rental company was trying to reach me to confirm my reservation for the SUV to Tucson. I was trying to reach the real estate agent, and he was leaving messages saying the owner wasn't sure about us as renters, since our finances were so weak. It seemed pretty clear to me I was headed to Tucson. The only thing that wasn't clear was what method of suicide I would choose once I got there.

It didn't help that in LA we were in the midst of a two-week-long heat wave, as if Tucson were already invading my space. Added to that was the large billboard I passed every time I visited the house in Arcadia, the one advertising the new Hyundai Tucson model.

Sunday morning arrived, and the real estate agent told me the house was ours. We could move in on Monday. Cleaners would be preparing the house for us later that day. A huge sigh of relief, followed by a surge of panic. How in the world would we be able to afford the place? Even greater than that, though, was the elation at knowing the cats would be safe.

Sunday night the heat wave broke, just as I was handed the keys to our new home. An unexpected storm suddenly swept the area, filling the skies with lightning and soaking the sweltering streets with rain. I moved three cats at a time in new cat carriers I had purchased. The change at hand had finally arrived, and the upheaval that the cats had sensed all week had now begun to disrupt their lives.

After a few days, we had begun to settle in, though everything still felt foreign. The cats were in hiding, which was to be expected. Except for Tiny, who, being the courageous cat she is, stayed by us, mostly cuddling next to me. Scared but seemingly confident in us. As if to say, whatever you've chosen for us must be the right decision. I wished I could've been so sure.

Charlie never adapted. He was traumatized from the start and never recovered. Sophie and I knew this wasn't going to work for him. We reflected on Camila and what she had said about the tabby she once loved. At exactly the same moment, Sophie and I looked into each other's eyes and blurted, "Maybe she'll take Charlie!"

We needed to bring her cat food anyway, so we headed for her house. She listened to our idea but shook her head no. She had diabetes and it was hard enough just to take care of herself, without the added pressure of having a cat indoors. Especially one that would cry constantly if not let in or out on time. But she would make sure to take extra good care of him if we decided to return him to the colony. She looked at us carefully and added, "But he will miss you terribly." We nodded yes, that was true, but so would his colony family. His mother was there, his lover, his cousins. As we were talking, it was clear the decision had already been made.

I drove back to Arcadia and picked up Charlie. He moaned and screamed, not enjoying another move so soon after the last one. I kept telling him, "You're going to love where you're going. You don't know it yet, but you're going to love it." As we pulled into the driveway, he looked around from inside the carrying cage, recognizing his old stomping grounds. He lit up, excited. I lifted him from his carrier, and he leaped away, running to his waiting family and seeming immediately at home.

All the cats but Tiny remained in shock and hidden at our new home. She would walk with me through the foreign gardens, experiencing all the new sights and smells. She'd courageously go exploring a few feet ahead of me, then turn, and with her familiar high trill of recognition at seeing my face, run back to me for assurance that everything was okay.

I began making the trip back to the old neighborhood, calling the cats with the click of my tongue they had become so used to. The first few nights, nobody showed. Then Charlie, Caliby, and Baby Gray came running. Even Hyena sat perched nearby, his coat full of luster. I had brought snacks for them. Tears welled up as I watched them enjoy the treats. They looked well fed and healthy. Perhaps this was going to work. Maybe they would be cared for after all.

Like a dream come true, our cats now have complete freedom in the spacious, enclosed backyard of our new home, without the need for body harnesses or leashes. When I lounge in the grass, the three sisters come along and rest next to me. Previously impossible to capture once they had escaped, now they prefer to remain within arm's reach. Pierre slowly bats her eyes at me as she sits, almost tauntingly, as if trivializing all those sleepless nights I spent worrying about her when she was a fugitive outside. Tiny sits nearby, as does Gumdrop.

Peacocks roost in our yard with their young during the day, but the cats keep a respectful distance. They're preoccupied with racing across the lawn at full speed, leaping onto tall sycamore trees and dashing through Japanese maple groves. It's paradise for them. Now they don't sleep because they're bored; they sleep from exhaustion.

We only have the house for six months and don't know what the future holds beyond that. But I can't think about that now. In fact, if this is as good as the cats ever have it — as good as any of us ever has it — it's plenty.

Tiny and I taking a nap.

19 Present Day

O ur experience really has been a suburban incarnation of the roles cats and humans have played for millennia. Semiwild felines made their way on the edge of domestic life, and when it was found that they had utility, they were given a modicum of shelter and protection. My cats' ancestors lived around the granaries of ancient Egypt and Mesopotamia, and later prowled the alleyways and hidden places in cities from Jericho to London. Over generations, many were domesticated.

Another ancestral history of my colony runs parallel to this — cats as sacred, cats as holy, cats as magical creatures, cats as occult familiars, cats as fortune-tellers and soothsayers. In some cultures, cats are revered and exalted; in others, they are reviled and distrusted. In most cultures, they are imbued with power and otherness, and appreciated for a stubborn independence that is part of their nature. They are not loyal or easily trained like dogs. They can seem utterly indifferent to us, implacable and willful. There is a hint of wildness in even the most domestic of cats. They have been portrayed as cunning, selfish, and stealthy. They have also represented a kind of feminine beauty and power, sleek and agile and breathtakingly beautiful.

My love affair with the colony made me challenge my notions of love and family. I got involved with them when I was middle-aged, childless, and single. These cats became my family. They awoke in me the human impulse to help and protect, to serve and remain vulnerable. They showed me a path to meaning and fulfillment as I opened my heart to a group of ragged outsiders living on the margins of our so-called civilized world.

Nature has run its course, and the outside colony now consists of but six remaining cats: Snow White, Baby Gray, Caliby, Beige, Marble, and Charlie. Just as FixNation predicted, our colony has indeed dwindled significantly in size — naturally. Did my involvement help or harm these cats? I have no way of knowing. But it put my mind at ease, knowing I tried my best to offer them a more comfortable and, at times, safer existence, which enabled them to reach life spans well beyond what is considered normal for feral cats.

Yes, there were fires to put out and lives to save, a crisis around every corner. But being completely committed and engaged had its own rewards. Though it seems counterintuitive, by putting the cats' well-being ahead of my own, by not being constantly self-referential, I found myself deeply fulfilled. Content. This story really is about how a colony of feral cats adopted me and changed my life for the better.

I can make no sense of why some of our cats survived while

others did not. And particularly why those that lost their lives met their demise in such a violent manner. But it seems the way of things, not uncommon to beings everywhere and always, and probably unlikely to change. I have no answers. I just tried to make a difference for those in our care, and I wish the best for those still in the wild.

I haven't returned to Nepal or India. But I did take a brief trip to Pakistan and Azerbaijan with friends who were doing business there. We flew on Azerbaijan Airlines to Baku, the country's capital. The old, obviously underserviced Aeroflot plane clearly had had the name of the airline quickly splashed across its side when the post-Soviet states gained their independence. Whatever jets happened to be on the tarmac when the Soviet Union fell were simply claimed by the new republics as their own and repainted. As soon as I sat in my seat, I knew I was in trouble. No seatbelts. No flight attendants. Only one bolt secured my seat to the ground, causing it to swing widely into the aisle with the slightest provocation.

I decided the only way I would be able to keep my seat from moving was to recline. And recline I did, right into the lap of the person behind me. Nothing held my seat up, no matter what direction I moved. Looking over my shoulder, I could see that the stench I had been smelling was coming from overflowing toilets. The lavatories had no doors. The nonsmoking flight was soon so thick with cigarette and cigar smoke I could barely see out my window.

But in the middle of that frigid December night, through the snow flying past my window, I made out a large city below. I was surprised we were already arriving. I thought it would take us at least a few more hours. Studying the lights carefully, I saw that they didn't remain static. They would grow in intensity and then wane, then grow and wane. I found out later we had been flying over the war zone of Armenia and Azerbaijan and what I was seeing were bombs exploding.

After a few hours, we began our descent into Baku, the capital. People began lining the aisle, even though we were still hurling through the air at 250 mph. I couldn't wait to see what would happen when we landed. As expected, the entire line of people fell against one another like a plane full of dominoes, leveling everyone. I just wondered about the last person in line, up against the putrid lavatory.

The middle of the night. Frigid. Snow everywhere. The airport completely deserted. What had happened to everyone who was on the flight? Walking outside, not a soul. No taxis or buses. No sign of the sprawling city of Baku. Just the occasional gas flare explosion from oil refineries piercing the pitch-black sky. We had landed in hell. In winter. Finally a solitary black car creaked its way to the airport, eventually stopping in front of me. Peering through the only piece of intact glass in his otherwise pulverized safety-glass windshield, he yelled at us, "Baku! Baku!" What choice did we have? While regaling us with a passionate story in Russian, between deep swigs from a bottle of vodka glued to his nonsteering hand, and punching me in the chest for emphasis, he somehow made his way to Baku, occasionally spinning 360s on the black ice and hitting snowbanks like a bumper car.

But I digress. My last trip to Asia. A brief stop in Pakistan. While wandering the hills near the Khyber Pass, a friend and I happened on a weapons bazaar. The *New York Times* has since called this area "the most dangerous place in the world." Weapons of all types were on display and for sale here. Behind the tables of weapons stood a massive reinforced wall. It was into this wall that one would test weapons before purchasing them. What were the requirements for purchasing? Cash. Nothing else.

Amazed at what I was seeing, I was even more stunned when suddenly my very good friend, my best friend really, thick as thieves, like two peas in a pod, threw me into the crowd and yelled, "Salman Rushdie!"

In retrospect, it's damn funny. But at the time, given that everyone was armed, and that there was still a fatwa demanding Rushdie's execution, and, most important, the most important part of all, that I look identical to him, it was a dicey few moments. Heads turning slowly, rabid looks, guns being lowered, then just as suddenly, peals of laughter, the entire bazaar realizing the joke. Roars, people in hysterics.

Back home, all my screenplays remain unproduced. I wrote the smuggler story as a novella but thus far have had no bites. I still live my life as a hypocrite, saving cats but eating meat, caring about the environment but driving an exhaust-belching car, aspiring to be kind to others but cursing them under my breath.

Tiny sits on my chest as I write these last words. I still marvel that the universe entrusted this creature to someone as reckless as me.

I've never felt as strong a connection with any living being before. We've bonded more deeply than ever. She is the breath in my lungs, the true purpose of my life. I had always hoped I could completely surrender myself at least once to someone, and I have. I just never knew it would be a cat. I often repeat to her the mantra we used to say when she was young, and barely alive: "We hope you live forever."

Because, I admit it, I'm a cat lover.

Acknowledgments

First I must thank my parents, Ned and Sue. To give you a sense of how remarkable they are, when I was growing up, and even today, people would befriend me just so they could spend time with them. And they're the ones who urged me to write down stories of my cats. Especially my father, who strongly disagreed with my assessment that nobody would care to read about a bunch of wild cats in my backyard.

A special thanks to my sister Miriam, a talented writer and woman of deep compassion, a true port of solace in a challenging world.

To Kenneth Wapner, a multitalented literary professional and compassionate friend who helped sculpt the first version of the proposal and never wavered in his enthusiasm for the material. Anyone lucky enough to work with Ken should count their blessings.

Anne Depue is a writer's dream literary agent. Her genuine warmth, creative mind, and passion for books are complemented by her quick wit and expertise as a writer, editor, and of course skilled saleswoman. Thank you, Anne!

Deepest appreciation to Georgia Hughes, editorial director at New World Library. A true gem in the publishing world. This book couldn't have found a better home. And to Tracy Cunningham, who worked magic with my photographs of the cats for the chapter openings. The entire production, editorial, and marketing team at New World is without parallel, especially the work of Kristen Cashman, who put a polish on the manuscript that made it shine. A special thank-you to Mark Colucci for his patient and precise copyediting work.

Finally, most heartfelt thanks to the many unsung heroes, the feral-cat caregivers, vets and their assistants, understanding neighbors, and volunteers at shelters. People who choose to make a little space in their already busy lives to ensure these animals feel like they belong here too, and for helping make their lives just a little more comfortable.

Notes

Prologue

Page xiv *"There is no reciprocity"*: Margalit Fox, "Alice Thomas Ellis Dies at 72; Writer about Spiritual and Mundane," *New York Times*, March 12, 2005, www.nytimes.com/2005/03/12/books/alice-thomas-ellis-dies -at-72-writer-about-spiritual-and-mundane.html?_r=0.

Chapter 1: Welcome to LA

Page 4 *fifty thousand or so screenplays*: Scott Meslow, "How Hollywood Chooses Scripts: The Insider List That Led to 'Abduction,'" *Atlantic*, September 23, 2011, www.theatlantic.com/entertainment/archive /2011/09/how-hollywood-chooses-scripts-the-insider-list-that-led -to-abduction/245541.

Chapter 5: Sleepless in SoCal

Page 37 *"One day some people came"*: This story appears in different forms in various books and online. This version is paraphrased from the one found in Mark Epstein, "Freud and Buddha," Network of Spiritual Progressives, accessed February 26, 2016, http://spiritualprogressives.org /newsite/?p=651.

Page 39 *They migrated from their*: The Cat Encyclopedia: The Definitive Visual Guide (London: DK, 2014), 11–12.

Page 39 *graves discovered in Cyprus and Jericho*: Carlos A. Driscoll et al., "The Taming of the Cat," *Scientific American*, June 2009, 71.

Chapter 6: Intervention

Page 49 *"And remember the night"*: Rudyard Kipling, "The Law of the Jungle," in *The Second Jungle Book*, Project Gutenberg, last modified January 8, 2013, www.gutenberg.org/files/1937/1937-h/1937-h.htm.

Page 54 *Feral cats have been blamed*: "Threatened Species Strategy," Department of the Environment, Australian Government, accessed February 26, 2016, www.environment.gov.au/biodiversity/threatened/publications/threatened-species-strategy.

Page 54 *the representative supposedly replied*: James McDonald, "Kill Them All…," in "Cathars and Cathar Beliefs in the Languedoc: Cathar Church v Catholic Church v Waldensian Church," last modified September 15, 2014, www.cathar.info/cathar_catholic.htm#killthemall, citing Caesarius of Heisterbach, *Dialogus miraculorum*, ed. Joseph Strange (Cologne: Heberle, 1851), 2:296–98.

Page 55 *their origins in ancient Egypt*: M. Oldfield Howey, *The Cat in Magic and Myth* (Mineola, NY: Dover, 2003), 107.

Page 55 *the Episcopal Inquisition*: Donald W. Engels, *Classical Cats: The Rise and Fall of the Sacred Cat* (New York: Routledge, 2001), 2.

Page 55 *"Be fruitful and multiply"*: Genesis 1:28, New Revised Standard Version.

Page 55 *If they could not be subdued*: "The History of Human-Animal Interaction — the Medieval Period," Library Index, accessed February 27, 2016, www.libraryindex.com/pages/2149/History-Human-Animal-Interaction-MEDIEVAL-PERIOD.html; "Why Cats Were Hated in Medieval Europe," October 2, 2013, www.medievalists.net/2013/10/02/why-cats-were-hated-in-medieval-europe/.

Page 55 *when all God-fearing beasts*: Sarah Hartwell, "Feline Folktails — Cats in Folklore and Superstition," accessed February 27, 2016, http://messybeast.com/folktails.htm.

Page 55 *"The devyl playeth ofte"*: "Why Cats Were Hated."

Page 55 *The hairs at the tips*: Hartwell, "Feline Folktails."

Page 57 *"Were you scared up there?"*: Script of *Get Shorty*, accessed April 2, 2016, www.scifiscripts.com/msol/get_shorty.txt.

Page 60 *The story goes*: Adapted from Abhishek Joshi, "Yudhisthira's Dog — Tale from Mahabharat," *Dog with Blog*, August 27, 2014, http://dogwithblog.in/yudhisthiras-dog-tale-from-mahabharat/.

Page 60 *The spiritual master Kukkuripa*: Keith Dowman, *Masters of Mahamudra: Songs and Histories of the Eighty-Four Buddhist Siddhas* (Albany: State University of New York Press, 1985), 199.

Page 62 *According to local legend*: Madison Most, "The Concrete Jungle:

Uncovering the Mystery of Wild Parrots in Southern California," Havasi Wilderness Foundation, October 25, 2012, www.havasiwf.org /the-concrete-jungle-uncovering-the-mystery-of-wild-parrots-in -southern-california/.

Page 62   *aspiring to homogenization*: J. P., "We Have No Bananas Today," *Feast and Famine* (blog), *Economist*, February 27, 2014, www.economist .com/blogs/feastandfamine/2014/02/bananas.

Page 63   *Negative influences seem*: Roy F. Baumeister et al., "Bad Is Stronger Than Good," *Review of General Psychology* 5, no. 4 (2001): 323–70.

Page 63   *John Gottman*: Manie Bosman, "You Might Not Like It, but Bad Is Stronger Than Good," Strategic Leadership Institute, August 1, 2012, www.strategicleadershipinstitute.net/news/you-might-not-like-it-but -bad-is-stronger-than-good/.

Page 64   *"If you bring forth"*: Gospel of Thomas, saying 70.

Chapter 8: Supporting My New Family

Page 84   *we hope to be praised*: "A Piece of Teaching by Tilopa to Naropa," Long Live His Holiness the Dalai Lama, October 7, 2010, www.llhhdl.org /forum/topics/a-piece-of-teaching-by-tilopa.

Chapter 9: The Naming of Cats

Page 88   *"The Lord God said"*: Genesis 2:18–20, New Revised Standard Version.

Page 89   *"Now, you people have names"*: Neil Gaiman, *Coraline* (London: Bloomsbury, 2002; reprint, 2013), 45.

Page 98   *The rare male calico*: Laura Moss, "Why Are Male Calico Cats So Rare?," Mother Nature Network, February 4, 2015, www.mnn.com /family/pets/stories/why-are-male-calico-cats-so-rare.

Chapter 10: From the Fertile Crescent to Hello Kitty

Page 101   *Ten thousand years ago*: "The Natural History of the Cat," Alley Cat Allies, accessed February 27, 2016, www.alleycat.org/CatHistory.

Page 101   *cats as indoor pets*: Ibid.

Page 102   *approximately one hundred million*: David A. Jessup, "The Welfare of Feral Cats and Wildlife," *Journal of the American Veterinary Medical Association* 225, no. 9 (2004): 1377, http://abcbirds.org/wp-content /uploads/2015/07/Jessup-2004-Welfare-of-feral-cats-and-wildlife.pdf.

Page 102   *"wherever five or more cats"*: Durant Imboden, "Torre Argentina

Cat Sanctuary," accessed April 2, 2016, http://europeforvisitors.com /rome/sights/torre-argentina-cat-sanctuary.htm.

Page 102   *three hundred thousand feral cats*: Judy J., "Torre Argentina Cat Sanctuary," *Colony Chronicles* 2, no. 4 (2009): 4, www.forgottenfelines offorsyth.org/newslettervol2issue4page4.htm.

Page 102   *Rome's city council*: "History," Torre Argentina Roman Cat Sanctuary, accessed February 27, 2016, www.romancats.com/torreargentina /en/history.php.

Page 102   *In the very place*: Ibid.; Sylvia Poggioli, "Cat Fight in Rome: Beloved Shelter Faces Closure," NPR, December 4, 2012, www.npr.org /2012/12/04/166067815/cat-fight-in-rome-beloved-shelter-faces -closure.

Page 102   *Mere humans couldn't own*: Gloria Stephens, *Legacy of the Cat: The Ultimate Illustrated Guide* (San Francisco: Chronicle Books, 2001), 6.

Page 103   *Now that cats had attained*: R. Roger Breton and Nancy J. Creek, "The Cat in History," accessed April 2, 2016, www2.pvc.maricopa. edu/~cis233/CBrown/Final/cathistory[1].html.

Page 103   *Displays of grief*: Joshua J. Mark, "Cats in the Ancient World," *Ancient History Encyclopedia*, November 17, 2012, www.ancient.eu /article/466.

Page 103   *Should a house catch fire*: Stephens, *Legacy of the Cat*, 6.

Page 103   *Though it was illegal*: Ibid., 7.

Page 103   *A government department*: Mark, "Cats in the Ancient World."

Page 104   *the black plague wiped out*: Ole J. Benedictow, "The Black Death: The Greatest Catastrophe Ever," *History Today* 55, no. 3 (2005), www.historytoday.com/ole-j-benedictow/black-death-greatest -catastrophe-ever.

Page 104   *Pope Gregory IX*: "The History of Human-Animal Interaction — the Medieval Period," Library Index, accessed February 27, 2016, www.libraryindex.com/pages/2149/History-Human-Animal -Interaction-MEDIEVAL-PERIOD.html; L. A. Vocelle, "History of the Cat in the Middle Ages (Part 2)," The Great Cat, February 8, 2013, www.thegreatcat.org/history-of-the-cat-in-the-middle-ages-part-2.

Page 104   *Pope Innocent VIII*: Wendy Christensen, *The Humane Society of the United States Complete Guide to Cat Care* (New York: St. Martin's Griffin, 2004), 14.

Page 104   *This current of thought*: Edward Slowik, "Descartes' Physics," *Stanford Encyclopedia of Philosophy*, last modified July 18, 2013, http://plato.stanford.edu/entries/descartes-physics.

Page 105   *Descartes posits*: Gary Steiner, *Anthropocentrism and Its Discontents:*

The Moral Status of Animals in the History of Western Thought (Pittsburgh, PA: University of Pittsburgh Press, 2005), 13–19; Tom Regan and Peter Singer, eds., *Animal Rights and Human Obligations*, 2nd ed. (Englewood Cliffs, NJ: Prentice Hall, 1989), 4–5, 60.

Page 105 *those illegally hiding cats*: Holle Abee, "Cats and the Black Plague," HubPages, last modified February 4, 2010, http://hubpages.com /education/Cats-and-the-Black-Plague.

Page 105 *Laws enacted*: Ibid.

Page 105 *"When I play with my cat"*: Michel de Montaigne, "Apology for Raimond Sebond," in *Essays of Michel de Montaigne*, ed. William Carew Hazlitt, trans. Charles Cotton, Project Gutenberg, last modified September 5, 2012, www.gutenberg.org/files/3600/3600-h/3600-h.htm, bk. 2, chap. 12.

Page 106 *Hundreds of years before*: Bruce Fogle, *The Encyclopedia of the Cat* (New York: DK, 1997), 118.

Page 106 *After arriving in Britain*: "Freyja and Her Cats," accessed February 27, 2016, www.freyjafirst.com/Cats.aspx; "Viking Pets and Domesticated Animals," Viking Answer Lady, last modified February 27, 2016, www.vikinganswerlady.com/vik_pets.shtml.

Page 106 *The Danes also held*: "Breed Spotlight: Norwegian Forest Cat," NSW Cat Fanciers Association, accessed February 27, 2016, www.nswcfa.asn.au/index.php?page=breeds.

Page 106 *accompanied Christopher Columbus*: "Animals," Mariners' Museum, accessed February 27, 2016, http://ageofex.marinersmuseum.org /?type=webpage&id=46.

Page 106 *Louis XIV required*: Katharine M. Rogers, *The Cat and the Human Imagination: Feline Images from Bast to Garfield* (Ann Arbor: University of Michigan Press, 1998), 72.

Page 106 *During the European colonization*: Sarah Hartwell, "Polydactyl Cats (Part 1)," accessed April 2, 2016, http://messybeast.com /poly-cats.html.

Page 107 *Even the U.S. Naval Institute*: "Cats in the Sea Services," U.S. Naval Institute, accessed February 27, 2016, www.usni.org/news-and -features/cats-and-the-sea-services.

Page 107 *The symbiotic relationship*: Patrick Roberts, "Cats in Wartime," *Featuring Felines*, accessed February 27, 2016, www.purr-n-fur.org.uk /featuring/war02.html.

Page 107 *Keeping rodents under control*: "Cats in the Sea Services."

Page 107 *It began as analytical*: "Strange at Sea: Maritime Myths and

Superstitions," Odyssey Marine Exploration, accessed February 27, 2016, www.shipwreck.net/oid/Nov12-maritimesuperstitions.php.

Page 107   *In March 1943*: "Maizie, the Cat, Keeps Men Sane," *Spokesman-Review*, June 22, 1943, https://news.google.com/newspapers?id =eR1WAAAAIBAJ&sjid=WuQDAAAAIBAJ&pg=1966%2C1726056.

Page 107   *The British frigate*: Patrick Roberts, "Simon, of HMS *Amethyst*," *Featuring Felines*, accessed February 27, 2016, www.purr-n-fur.org.uk /famous/simon.html.

Page 108   *Another cat, named U-boat*: Ashley Morgan, *Wonder Cats: True Stories of Extraordinary Felines* (Chichester, UK: Summersdale, 2010), 47.

Page 108   *Some mariners believed*: "Strange at Sea."

Page 108   *According to another*: Ibid.

Page 108   *RMS* Empress of Ireland: Alastair Walker, *Four Thousand Lives Lost: The Inquiries of Lord Mersey into the Sinking of the* Titanic, *the* Empress of Ireland, *the* Falaba *and the* Lusitania (Stroud, UK: History Press, 2012); "RMS Empress of Ireland (1906)," Project Gutenberg, accessed February 27, 2016, http://central.gutenberg.org/articles /RMS_Empress_of_Ireland_(1906).

Page 109   *An homage to ship cats*: "Jones (Cat)," *Xenopedia*, accessed February 27, 2016, http://avp.wikia.com/wiki/Jones_(cat); "Jonesy," *Alien Anthology Wiki*, accessed February 27, 2016, http://alienanthology. wikia.com/wiki/Jonesy.

Page 109   *Cats ingratiated themselves*: Lorraine Chittock, *Cats of Cairo: Egypt's Enduring Legacy* (New York: Abbeville Press, 2001).

Page 109   *They were particularly revered*: Nuha N. N. Khoury, "Cat," in *Encyclopedia of Islam*, ed. Juan E. Campo (New York: Facts on File, 2009), http://ashtoncentralmosque.com/wp-content/uploads/2014/07 /Encyclopedia-of-Islam-by-Juan-Campo.pdf, p. 182.

Page 109   *who wrote odes to cats*: www.muslimheritage.com/article/cats -islamic-culture, accessed April 22, 2016.

Page 109   *Their purrs were compared*: Cem Nizamoglu, "Cats in Islamic Culture," Foundation for Science, Technology and Civilisation, accessed February 27, 2016, www.muslimheritage.com/article/cats -islamic-culture.

Page 109   *Most cat purrs fall within*: Elizabeth von Muggenthaler, "The Felid Purr: A Bio-mechanical Healing Mechanism," Fauna Communications Research Institute, accessed February 27, 2016, www.animalvoice.com /catpurrP.htm.

Page 109   *David Hawkins's calibration list*: Nancy Bragin, "Dr. David Hawkins Calibrated List," *Blissful Blog*, December 29, 2012,

http://nancybragin.com/2012/12/29/dr-david-hawkins-calibrated
-reading-list/.

Page 110 *"The grammarian Ibn Babshad"*: Chittock, *Cats of Cairo*, 40.

Page 110 *Another story is told*: Muhammad Sajad Ali, "The Sunnah and
Blessings in Healing Effects of Cats: Cat Purr Frequency Increases Bone
Density & Speeds Injury Recovery," March 20, 2010, www.deenislam
.co.uk/cats.htm.

Page 110 *Muhammad was said to*: "The Love and Importance of Cats in
Islam," February 15, 2013, http://islam.ru/en/content/story/love
-and-importance-cats-islam.

Page 111 *Whether or not Muhammad actually said*: Annemarie Schimmel,
Deciphering the Signs of God: A Phenomenological Approach to Islam
(Albany: State University of New York Press, 1994), 23; Georgie Anne
Geyer, *When Cats Reigned Like Kings: On the Trail of the Sacred Cats*
(Kansas City: Andrews McMeel, 2004), 28; 'Abdullah bin 'Umar, hadith,
vol. 3, bk. 40, no. 553.

Page 111 *Muhammad even gave*: Nizamoglu, "Cats in Islamic Culture."

Page 111 *Abu's kitten saved*: Schimmel, *Deciphering the Signs of God*, 23.

Page 111 *differently in Christian folklore*: "Tabby Cat," accessed February 27,
2016, http://domesticcatworld.com/tabby-cat; Sarah Hartwell, "Feline
Folktails — Cats in Folklore and Superstition," accessed February 27,
2016, http://messybeast.com/folktails.htm.

Page 112 *"The Chinese goddess Li Shou"*: www.playfulkitty.net/2014/01/27
/cats-in-history-chinese-truth-and-mythology, accessed on April 22,
2016; http://messybeast.com/moggycat/chinese.htm, accessed on
April 22, 2016; www.ancient.eu/article/466, accessed on April 22, 2016.

Page 112 *There is a small cat shrine*: Ella Morton, "Tashirojima: The Japanese
Island Ruled by Cats," *Atlas Obscura* (blog), *Slate*, May 15, 2014, www
.slate.com/blogs/atlas_obscura/2014/05/15/tashirojima_is_an_island
_in_japan_ruled_by_cats.html.

Page 113 *legend of the* bakeneko: Matthew Meyer, "Bakeneko," accessed
February 27, 2016, http://yokai.com/bakeneko/.

Page 113 *"popular cult of* maneki-neko": www.catchannel.com/magazines
/catfancy/december-2006/maneki-neko.aspx; www.catster.com
/lifestyle/maneki-neko-fortune-cat-5-interesting-facts, accessed on
April 22, 2016; Shizuko Mishima, "Introduction to Manekineko,"
accessed February 27, 2016, http://gojapan.about.com/cs/tradition
culture/a/luckycats.htm.

Page 113 *inspired by Lewis Carroll's*: Cheong Suk-Wai, "Still Money in the
Kitty," *New Straits Times*, December 2, 2003, https://news.google.com

/newspapers?id=goAhAAAAIBAJ&sjid=v3sFAAAAIBAJ&pg
=1278%2C1550703.

Page 113 *but ironically Hello Kitty*: Jean Trinh, "Sanrio's Shocking Reveal:
Hello Kitty Is NOT a Cat," *LAist*, August 27, 2014, http://laist
.com/2014/08/27/sanrios_shocking_reveal_hello_kitty.php.

Chapter 11: Protecting the Colony

Page 121 *The visiting Greek historian*: www.ancient.eu/article/466 and
www.catmuseumsf.org/egyptcats.html, accessed on April 21, 2016.
Page 122 *"The greatest example"*: Joshua J. Mark, "Cats in the Ancient World,"
Ancient History Encyclopedia, November 17, 2012, www.ancient.eu
/article/466.

Chapter 12: Interrupting the Cycle

Page 128 *Disneyland's feral-cat colony*: "TNR at Work — Disneyland Finds
Balance with Feral Cats," Alley Cat Allies, accessed February 27, 2016,
www.alleycat.org/page.aspx?pid=873.
Page 129 *"Feral Cats: They live in"*: Feral Cat Rescue, *A Walk on the Wild
Side* 1 (December 2012), www.feralcatrescuemd.org/uploads/2012
_FCR_email_newsletter.pdf, pp. 1, 8.
Page 129 *Stanford University Cat Network*: "Trap-Neuter-Return," Feral Cat
Assistance Program, accessed February 27, 2016, http://fcap.homestead
.com/trapneuterreturn.html.
Page 129 *Southern Animal Foundation*: Ibid.
Page 134 *"Decades of studies prove"*: "Biology and Behavior of the Cat,"
Alley Cat Allies, accessed March 13, 2016, www.alleycat.org/Cat
Biology.
Page 134 *In areas devoid of rodents*: Cats and Predation, Alley Cat Rescue,
accessed February 27, 2016, www.saveacat.org/uploads/4/8/4/1
/48413975/cats_and_predation.pdf, p. 3.
Page 134 *"almost always catch"*: Ibid.
Page 134 *"It is likely that most"*: "Are Cats Causing Bird Declines?," Royal
Society for the Protection of Birds, accessed February 27, 2016,
www.rspb.org.uk/makeahomeforwildlife/advice/gardening
/unwantedvisitors/cats/birddeclines.aspx.
Page 138 *Which is why articles*: Tabitha M. Powledge, "Why Does Your Cat
Love You…Sort Of? DNA Unravels Feline Mysteries," Genetic Liter-
acy Project, November 18, 2014, www.geneticliteracyproject.org/2014

/11/18/why-does-your-cat-love-you-sort-of-dna-unravels-feline
-mysteries/.

Page 138   *Dogs have a jump*: Alicia Ault, "Ask Smithsonian: Are Cats Domesticated?," Smithsonian.com, April 30, 2015, www.smithsonianmag.com
/smithsonian-institution/ask-smithsonian-are-cats-domesticated
-180955111/?no-ist.

Page 138   *And while cat genome sequencing*: Ibid.

Page 138   *Most would likely not survive*: Ibid.

Page 138   *Some scientists go so far*: Ibid.

Page 139   *"I think what confuses"*: Ferris Jabr, "Are Cats Domesticated?," *New
Yorker*, October 23, 2015, www.newyorker.com/tech/elements
/are-cats-domesticated.

Chapter 13: Three Sisters

Page 155   *One of the ancient Hindu*: Swami Nikhilananda, trans., "Mandukya
Upanishad with Gaudapada's Karika," chap. 2, v. 17 [of Gaudapada's
Karika], accessed February 27, 2016, www.swamij.com/upanishad
-mandukya-karika.htm; James Swartz, *Mandukya Upanishad: An Ancient
Sanskrit Text on the Nature of Reality*, accessed February 27, 2016,
shiningworld.com/site/files/pdfs/publications/scripture/mandukya
_upanishad_swartz.pdf.

Page 155   *"Cowards die many times"*: William Shakespeare, *Julius Caesar*, ed.
Philip Weller, 2.2.32–33, Shakespeare Navigators, accessed February 27,
2016, www.shakespeare-navigators.com/JC_Navigator/JC_2_2.html.

Chapter 14: Indoors and Out

Page 173   *A central belief*: Colleen Taylor Sen, *Food Culture in India* (West-
port, CT: Greenwood Press, 2004), 10.

Page 173   *Arya Asanga*: Alexander Berzin, "Overview of *Uttaratantra*" (tran-
script of lecture, Berlin, October 2005), Berzin Archives,
www.berzinarchives.com/web/en/archives/sutra/level6_study
_major_texts/uttaratantra/overview_of_uttaratantra/part_1.html.

Chapter 18: Moving

Page 202   *"Mother Nature doesn't"*: All information on the Working Cats Program in this chapter, including the quotes from Melya Kaplan, are from
Jerome Campbell, "Cats Rescued from Shelters Are Hired for Rodent

Patrol," *Los Angeles Times*, June 26, 2015, www.latimes.com/local /california/la-me-adv-cats-for-hire-20150627-story.html.
Page 204   *"You become responsible"*: Antoine de Saint Exupéry, *The Little Prince*, trans. Katherine Woods (New York: Harcourt, 1970), 48.

Chapter 19: Present Day

Page 220   *"the most dangerous place"*: Suroosh Alvi, "The Gun Markets of Pakistan," CNN, January 27, 2010, www.cnn.com/2010/WORLD /asiapcf/01/26/vbs.gun.markets.pakistan.

Resources

I 've included resources that I've used and might be helpful, and many of these websites offer links to other feral-cat resources. A quick online search would likely lead you to feral-cat organizations in your area.

Alley Cat Allies
7920 Norfolk Ave., #600
Bethesda, MD 20814
Website: www.alleycat.org
Phone: 240-482-1980
Fax: 240-482-1990

Feral Cat Caretakers' Coalition
PO Box 491244
Los Angeles, CA 90049
Website: www.feralcatcaretakers.org
Phone: 310-820-4122
Email: info@feralcatcaretakers.org

FixNation
7680 Clybourn Ave.
Los Angeles, CA 91352
Website: fixnation.org
Phone: 818-524-2287
Fax: 818-767-7791
Email (general): info@fixnation.org
Email (appointments): appointments@fixnation.org

Torre Argentina Cat Sanctuary
Mailing address:
Associazione Culturale Colonia Felina di Torre Argentina
via Marco Papio, 15
00175 Rome, Italy
Physical address:
Largo di Torre Argentina
via di Torre Argentina, 1
00186 Rome, Italy
(Corner of via Florida and via di Torre Argentina)
Phone (main): +39 06 68805611
Phone (cell): +39 340 9862294
Email: torreargentina@tiscali.it
Email (alternate): torreargentina@catsdb.com

Voice for the Animals Foundation
Mailing address:
2633 Lincoln Blvd., #202
Santa Monica, CA 90405
Website: www.vftafoundation.org
Phone: 310-392-5153
Fax: 310-773-9027
Email: info@vftafoundation.org

About the Author

Andrew Bloomfield is a longtime student of spiritual practices. He spent nearly two years in Nepal, where he followed a seventeenth-century pilgrim's guidebook to research spiritual sites around the lower Himalayas. He has worked as assistant manager and book buyer for East West Books in Manhattan and for Snow Lion Publications in Ithaca, New York. He opened his own bookstore, Infinity Books, in Pioneer Square in Seattle, where he hosted many public events, including appearances by renowned Tibetan lamas, Hindu saints, and Zen masters. He later moved to Los Angeles to work for a Vedic astrologer. Andrew is the author of *How to Practice Vedic Astrology* (with CD-ROM) and *Learning Practical Tibetan* (with MP3s).

**If you have stories about caring for a feral cat,
or a colony of ferals, that you'd like to share,
please send them to Andrew:
feralstory@gmail.com**